2nd Workshop on Syntax and Structure in Statistical Translation 2008

(SSST-2)

Held in conjunction with ACL-HLT 2008

Columbus, Ohio, USA
20 June 2008

Editors:

David Chiang **Dekai Wu**

ISBN: 978-1-61738-555-1

Printed from e-media with permission by:

Curran Associates, Inc.
57 Morehouse Lane
Red Hook, NY 12571

CURRAN ASSOCIATES INC. proceedings.com

Some format issues inherent in the e-media version may also appear in this print version.

Printed by Curran Associates, Inc. (2010)

For permission requests, please contact the Association for Computational Linguistics at the address below.

Association for Computational Linguistics
209 N. Eighth Street
Stroudsburg, Pennsylvania 18360

Phone: 1-570-476-8006
Fax: 1-570-476-0860

acl@aclweb.org

Additional copies of this publication are available from:

Curran Associates, Inc.
57 Morehouse Lane
Red Hook, NY 12571 USA
Phone: 845-758-0400
Fax: 845-758-2634
Email: curran@proceedings.com
Web: www.proceedings.com

Introduction

The Second Workshop on Syntax and Structure in Statistical Translation (SSST-2) was held on 20 June 2008 following the ACL-08: HLT conference hosted by Ohio State University in Columbus, Ohio. Like the first SSST workshop in 2007, it aimed to bring together researchers from different communities working in the rapidly growing field of statistical, tree-structured models of natural language translation.

We selected eleven papers for this year's workshop. There was a strong emphasis this year on the use of explicit syntactic information: constituent structures (Yamamoto, Okuma and Sumita; Zhou, Xiang, Zhu and Gao; Elming; Clark, Frederking and Levin; Lavie, Parlikar and Ambati), dependency structures (Nikoulina and Dymetman; Ma, Ozdowska, Sun and Way), part-of-speech tags (Tillmann), and combinations thereof (Ge, Ittycheriah and Papineni). These papers applied syntactic information to grammar-based models as well as to phrase-based and word-based models. The program was rounded out by papers describing new decoding techniques (Li and Khudanpur) and machine-learning techniques (Subotin) for grammar-based translation models.

We would like to thank our authors and our Program Committee for making this year's SSST workshop another success.

David Chiang and Dekai Wu[1]

[1]This work was supported in part by the Defense Advanced Research Projects Agency (DARPA) under GALE Contract Nos. HR0011-06-C-0023, subcontract SRI International (Dekai Wu) and HR0011-06-C-0022, subcontract BBN Technologies 9500008412 (David Chiang). Any opinions, findings and conclusions or recommendations expressed in this material are those of the author(s) and do not necessarily reflect the views of the Defense Advanced Research Projects Agency.

Organizers:

David CHIANG, USC Information Sciences Institute, USA
Dekai WU, Hong Kong University of Science and Technology (HKUST), Hong Kong

Program Committee:

Srinivas BANGALORE, AT&T Research, USA
Marine CARPUAT, Hong Kong University of Science and Technology (HKUST), Hong Kong
Pascale FUNG, Hong Kong University of Science and Technology (HKUST), Hong Kong
Daniel GILDEA, University of Rochester, USA
Kevin KNIGHT, USC Information Sciences Institute, USA
Jonas KUHN, University of Potsdam, Germany
Yang LIU, Institute of Computing Technology, Chinese Academy of Sciences, China
Daniel MARCU, USC Information Sciences Institute, USA
Yuji MATSUMOTO, Nara Institute of Science and Technology, Japan
Hermann NEY, RWTH Aachen, Germany
Owen RAMBOW, Columbia University, USA
Philip RESNIK, University of Maryland, USA
Stefan RIEZLER, Google Inc., USA
Libin SHEN, BBN Technologies, USA
Christoph TILLMANN, IBM T. J. Watson Research Center, USA
Stephan VOGEL, Carnegie Mellon University, USA
Taro WATANABE, NTT Communication Science Laboratories, Japan
Andy WAY, Dublin City University, Ireland
Yuk-Wah WONG, Google Inc., USA
Richard ZENS, Google Inc., USA

Table of Contents

Workshop Program

Friday, June 20, 2008

9:00–9:05 Opening Remarks

9:05–9:30 *Imposing Constraints from the Source Tree on ITG Constraints for SMT*
Hirofumi YAMAMOTO, Hideo OKUMA and Eiichiro SUMITA

9:30–9:55 *A Scalable Decoder for Parsing-Based Machine Translation with Equivalent Language Model State Maintenance*
Zhifei LI and Sanjeev KHUDANPUR

9:55–10:20 *Prior Derivation Models For Formally Syntax-Based Translation Using Linguistically Syntactic Parsing and Tree Kernels*
Bowen ZHOU, Bing XIANG, Xiaodan ZHU and Yuqing GAO

10:30–11:00 Coffee Break

11:00–11:25 *Generalizing Local Translation Models*
Michael SUBOTIN

11:25–12:15 Invited Talk

12:15–13:45 Lunch

13:45–14:10 *A Rule-Driven Dynamic Programming Decoder for Statistical MT*
Christoph TILLMANN

14:10–14:35 *Syntactic Reordering Integrated with Phrase-Based SMT*
Jakob ELMING

14:40–15:05 *Experiments in Discriminating Phrase-Based Translations on the Basis of Syntactic Coupling Features*
Vassilina NIKOULINA and Marc DYMETMAN

15:05–15:30 *Multiple Reorderings in Phrase-Based Machine Translation*
Niyu GE, Abe ITTYCHERIAH and Kishore PAPINENI

15:30–16:00 Coffee Break

Friday, June 20, 2008 (continued)

16:00–16:25 *Improving Word Alignment Using Syntactic Dependencies*
Yanjun MA, Sylwia OZDOWSKA, Yanli SUN and Andy WAY

16:25–16:50 *Inductive Detection of Language Features via Clustering Minimal Pairs: Toward Feature-Rich Grammars in Machine Translation*
Jonathan H. CLARK, Robert FREDERKING and Lori LEVIN

16:50–17:15 *Syntax-Driven Learning of Sub-Sentential Translation Equivalents and Translation Rules from Parsed Parallel Corpora*
Alon LAVIE, Alok PARLIKAR and Vamshi AMBATI

17:15–17:45 Panel Discussion

Imposing Constraints from the Source Tree on ITG Constraints for SMT

Hirofumi Yamamoto†,††,††† **Hideo Okuma†,††** **Eiichiro Sumita†,††**
†National Institute of Information and Communications Technology
/ 2-2-2 Hikaridai Seika-cho Soraku-gun Kyoto Japan
††ATR Spoken Language Communication Research Labs.
†††Kinki University School of Sience and Engineering Department of Information
{hirofumi.yamamoto,hideo.okuma,eiichiro.sumita}@nict.go.jp

Abstract

In current statistical machine translation (SMT), erroneous word reordering is one of the most serious problems. To resolve this problem, many word-reordering constraint techniques have been proposed. The inversion transduction grammar (ITG) is one of these constraints. In ITG constraints, target-side word order is obtained by rotating nodes of the source-side binary tree. In these node rotations, the source binary tree instance is not considered. Therefore, stronger constraints for word reordering can be obtained by imposing further constraints derived from the source tree on the ITG constraints. For example, for the source word sequence { a b c d }, ITG constraints allow a total of twenty-two target word orderings. However, when the source binary tree instance ((a b) (c d)) is given, our proposed "imposing source tree on ITG" (IST-ITG) constraints allow only eight word orderings. The reduction in the number of word-order permutations by our proposed stronger constraints efficiently suppresses erroneous word orderings. In our experiments with IST-ITG using the NIST MT08 English-to-Chinese translation track's data, the proposed method resulted in a 1.8-points improvement in character BLEU-4 (35.2 to 37.0) and a 6.2% lower CER (74.1 to 67.9%) compared with our baseline condition.

1 Introduction

Statistical methods are widely used for machine translation. One of the popular statistical machine translation paradigms is the phrase-based model (PBSMT) (Marcu et al., 2002; Koehn et al., 2003; Och et al., 2004). In PBSMT, errors in word reordering, especially in global reordering, are one of the most serious problems. Approaches used to resolve this problem are categorized into two types. The first type is linguistically syntax-based. In this approach, source (Quirk et al., 2005; Liu et al., 2006; Huang et al., 2006), target (Yamada et al., 2000; Galley et al., 2006; Marcu et al., 2006), or both side (Melamed 2004; Ding et al., 2005) tree structures are used for model training. The second type is formal constraints on word permutations. IBM constraints (Berger et al., 1996), lexical word reordering model (Tillmann, 2004), and inversion transduction grammar (ITG) constraints (Wu, 1995; Wu, 1997) belong to this type of approach. Our approach is an extension of ITG constraints and is a hybrid of the first and second type of approach.

We propose "imposing source tree on ITG" (IST-ITG) constraints for directly introducing source sentence structure into our set of constraints. In IST-ITG, ITG constraints under the given source sentence tree structure are used as stronger constraints than the original ITG. For example, IST-ITG allows only eight word orderings for a four-word sentence, even though twenty-two word orderings are possible with respect of in the original ITG constraints.

In Section 2, we present the proposed IST-ITG for word-based translation. In Section 3, the proposed method is extended to phrase-based translation. In Section 4, we present a real-time decoding algorithm for IST-ITG constraints. In Section 5, we give details of the experiments and present the results. Finally, in Section 6, we offer a summary and some concluding remarks.

Proceedings of the Second ACL Workshop on Syntax and Structure in Statistical Translation (SSST-2), pages 1–9,
ACL-08: HLT, Columbus, Ohio, USA, June 2008.

2 Imposing the Source Tree on ITG Constraints

First, we introduce three previous studies on word reordering constraints: IBM constraints; lexical reordering model; and ITG constraints. Here, we consider one-to-one word-aligned source and target language sentence pairs as the simplest cases.

2.1 IBM constraints

In this constraint, a distortion penalty is given in accordance with the gap between the previously and the currently translated words, which is represented as the following equation.

$$p_D = exp(-\sum_i d_i) \quad (1)$$

where d_i for each i is defined as:

$$d_i = abs(position(e_{i-1}) + 1 - position(e_i)) \quad (2)$$

where e_i represents the translated word from the ith source word f_i, $position(w)$ represents the position of the word w. Sometimes, a limit is set for d_i for similar language pairs such as French and English. However, for dissimilar language pairs, such as Japanese and English or Chinese and English, limiting d_i is not beneficial.

2.2 Lexical Reordering Model

In the lexical reordering model, reordering probabilities are assigned to each word pair $\{f_i, e_i\}$. Reordering positions are categorized into three types, monotone, swap, and discontinuous. The probability is assigned to left and right sides as $p_s(t|f_i, e_i)$, where, s is left (l) or right (r), t is monotone (m), swap (s), or discontinuous (d). Therefore, a total of six probabilities are assigned to each word pair. For the source word sub-sequence f_{i-1}, f_i, probabilities of target sub-sequences are calculated as follows:

- $p(e_{i-1}, e_i) = p_r(m|f_{i-1}, e_{i-1})p_l(m|f_i, e_i)$
- $p(e_i, e_{i-1}) = p_r(s|f_{i-1}, e_{i-1})p_l(s|f_i, e_i)$
- $p(otherwise) = p_r(d|f_{i-1}, e_{i-1})p_l(d|f_i, e_i)$

2.3 ITG Constraints

In one-to-one word-alignment, the source word f_i is translated into the target word e_i. The source sentence $[f_1, f_2, ..., f_N]$ is translated into a reordered sequence of word $[e_1, e_2, ..., e_N]$. The number of reorderings is $N!$. When ITG is introduced, this combination $N!$ can be reduced in accordance with the following constraints.

- All possible binary tree structures are generated from the source word sequence.
- The target sentence is obtained by rotating any node of the binary trees.

When $N = 4$, the ITG constraints can reduce the number of combinations from $4! = 24$ to 22 by rejecting combinations $[e_3, e_1, e_4, e_2]$ and $[e_2, e_4, e_1, e_3]$. For a 4-word sentence, the search space is reduced to 92%(22/24), but for 10-word sentence, the search space is only 6%(206,098/3,628,800) of the original full space.

2.4 Imposing Source Tree Constraints

In ITG constraints, the source-side binary tree instance is not considered. Therefore, if the source sentence binary tree is utilized, stronger constraints than the original ITG can be created. By parsing the source sentence, a parse tree is obtained. After parsing, a bracketed sentence is obtained by removing the node labels, and this bracketed sentence can be converted to a binary tree. For example, the parse tree, (S1 (S (NP (DT This)) (VP (AUX is) (NP (DT a) (NN pen))))), is obtained from the source sentence "This is a pen". By removing the node labels, a bracketed sentence ((This) ((is) ((a) (pen)))) is obtained. Such a bracketed sentence (equivalent to a binary tree) can be used to produce constraints. If IST-ITG is applied, the number of word orderings in $N = 4$ is reduced to 8, down from 22 with ITG. For example, for the source-side bracketed tree $((f_1\ f_2)(f_3\ f_4))$, eight target sequences $[e_1, e_2, e_3, e_4]$, $[e_2, e_1, e_3, e_4]$, $[e_1, e_2, e_4, e_3]$, $[e_2, e_1, e_4, e_3]$, $[e_3, e_4, e_1, e_2]$, $[e_3, e_4, e_2, e_1]$, $[e_4, e_3, e_1, e_2]$, and $[e_4, e_3, e_2, e_1]$ are accepted. For the source-side bracketed tree $(((f_1\ f_2)f_3)f_4)$, eight sequences $[e_1, e_2, e_3, e_4]$, $[e_2, e_1, e_3, e_4]$, $[e_3, e_1, e_2, e_4]$, $[e_3, e_1, e_2, e_4]$, $[e_4, e_1, e_2, e_3]$, $[e_4, e_2, e_1, e_3]$, $[e_4, e_3, e_1, e_2]$, and

$[e_4, e_3, e_2, e_1]$ are accepted. Generally, the number of word orderings is reduced to 2^{N-1}. Table 1 shows the number of word orderings in a target word sequence for each N with ITG, IST-ITG, and no constraints.

Table 1: Number of word orderings in each type of constraint

N	IST-ITG	ITG	No Constraint
1	1	1	1
2	2	2	2
3	4	6	6
4	8	22	24
5	16	90	120
6	32	394	720
7	64	1806	5040
8	128	8558	40320
9	256	41586	362880
10	512	206098	3628800
15	16384	745387038	1307674368000

2.5 Extension to Non-binary Tree

In the above subsection, a source binary tree was assumed in order to perform IST-ITG. However, parsing results sometimes are not binary trees. In this case, some tree nodes have more than two branches. For a non-binary node, any reordering of branches is allowed. In a non-binary tree $(f_1(f_2\ f_3\ f_4))$, twelve target-side sequences $[e_1, e_2, e_3, e_4]$, $[e_1, e_2, e_4, e_3]$, $[e_1, e_3, e_2, e_4]$, $[e_1, e_3, e_4, e_2]$, $[e_1, e_4, e_2, e_3]$, $[e_1, e_4, e_3, e_2]$, $[e_2, e_3, e_4, e_1]$, $[e_2, e_4, e_3, e_1]$, $[e_3, e_2, e_4, e_1]$, $[e_3, e_4, e_2, e_1]$, $[e_4, e_2, e_3, e_1]$, and $[e_4, e_3, e_2, e_1]$ are allowed. For nodes that have more than three branches, the original ITG constraints are locally applied. Therefore, for a non-binary tree $(f_1(f_2\ f_3\ f_4\ f_5))$, $22 \times 2 = 44$ word orderings are allowed in the target-side and represented by the following formula.

$$\prod_{i=1}^{n}(S_{Bi}) \tag{3}$$

where S_k represents the number of combinations from the original ITG constraints for $N = k$ and Bi represents the number of branches at the ith node.

3 IST-ITG in Phrase-based SMT

In the above section, we described each constraint in the case of a one-to-one word-alignment. In this section, we consider phrase-based models. When a phrase-based model is used, each constraint must be extended. For IBM constraints, equation (2) is rewritten using phrase Pe_n instead of word e_n as follows:

$$\begin{aligned} d_i &= abs(last\_position(Pe_{i-1}) + 1 \\ &\quad - first\_position(Pe_i)) \end{aligned} \tag{4}$$

where $last\_position(Pe_n)$ represents the position of the last word in nth phrase, and $first\_position(Pe_n)$ represents the position of the first word in nth phrase. The lexical reordering model and ITG constraints can be extended by changing the model (or constraint) unit from "word" to "phrase". However, in IST-ITG, "word" must be used for the constraint unit since the parse (bracketed tree) unit is in "words". To absorb different units between translation models and IST-ITG constraints, we investigated a new limitation for word ordering as follows.

- Word ordering that destroys a phrase is not allowed.

When this limitation is applied, the translated word ordering is obtained from the bracketed source sentence tree by reordering the nodes in the tree, the same as for one-to-one word-alignment. According to this limitation, the following nodes cannot be reordered. If a sub-tree with root node X includes part of a phrase ph, node X cannot be reordered. Consider the source bracketed source tree ((e_a e_b e_c) ((e_d e_e) (e_f e_g))), in which e_b e_c, and e_d form a phrase e_{ph} as in Figure 1. Node 1 cannot be reordered since part of the phrase e_b e_c is included in node 1's sub-tree. For the same reason, node 2 and 4 cannot be reordered. Node 3 can be reordered since the sub-tree does not include the phrase (target sequence $[f_a f_{ph} f_e f_g f_f]$ is obtained by rotating node 3). Node 5 also can be reordered since it includes the whole phrase (target sequence $[f_g f_f f_e f_{ph} f_a]$ is obtained by rotating node 5). If node 2 is reordered, phrase ph is split into two parts, and translated in two parts in the target sentence. It is inconsistent with the condition that phrase-to-phrase alignment is one-to-one. As a result, only the target sequences $[f_a f_{ph} f_e f_f f_g]$, $[f_a f_{ph} f_e f_g f_f]$, $[f_g f_f f_e f_{ph} f_a]$, and $[f_f f_g f_e f_{ph} f_a]$ are allowed. Here, f_{ph} represents an equivalent phrase in the translation for e_{ph}.

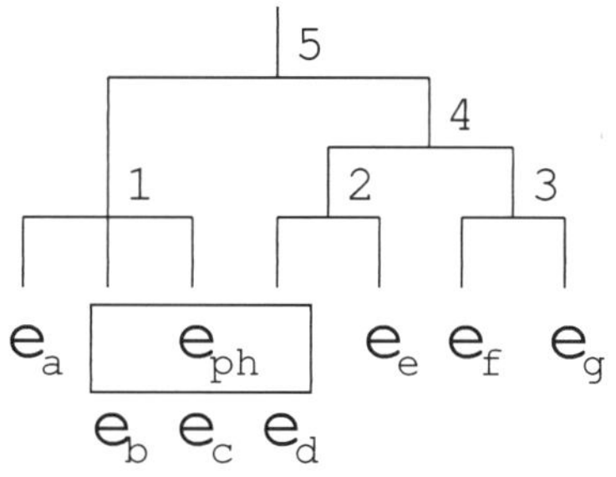

Figure 1: Example sentence tree with a phrase

4 Decoding with IST-ITG Constraints

In this section, we describe a one-pass decoding algorithm that uses IST-ITG constraints in the decoder. The translation target sentence is sequentially generated from left (sentence head) to right (sentence tail). To introduce the IST-ITG constraints into a decoder, the target candidate must be checked whether it satisfies the IST-ITG constraints or not whenever a new phrase is selected to extend a target candidate.

To explain this checking algorithm, we categorized source sub-trees into four types **UNTRANSLATED**, **TRANSLATED**, **TRANSLATING**, and **NG** (no good) as follows:

- If a sub-tree consists of only leaf word nodes, and all leaf words are not yet translated, this sub-tree is defined as **UNTRANSLATED**.
- If a sub-tree consists of only **UNTRANSLATED** sub-trees, this sub-tree is also **UNTRANSLATED**.
- If a sub-tree consists of only leaf word nodes, and all leaf words are already translated, this sub-tree is defined as **TRANSLATED**.
- If a sub-tree consists of only **TRANSLATED** sub-trees, this sub-tree is also **TRANSLATED**.
- If a sub-tree consists of only leaf word nodes with both translated and untranslated words, this sub-tree is defined as **TRANSLATING**.
- If a sub-tree consists of both **TRANSLATED** and **UNTRANSLATED** sub-trees, this sub-tree is **TRANSLATING**.
- If a sub-tree includes only one **TRANSLATING** sub-tree and any number (including zero) of **TRANSLATED** and **UNTRANSLATED** sub-trees, this sub-tree is **TRANSLATING**.
- If a sub-tree includes more than one **TRANSLATING** sub-tree, this sub-tree is **NG**.
- If a sub-tree includes **NG** sub-tree, this sub-tree is also **NG**.

If a translation candidate includes **TRANSLATING** sub-tree t, t must become **TRANSLATED** before anything else can happen. Given sub-tree $((ab)c)$, a is translated, b and c are not yet translated. In this case, b must be translated before c. If c is translated before b, the target word order becomes ACB. This word order does not satisfy the IST-ITG constraints. For the same reason, a candidate that includes an NG sub-tree does not satisfy the IST-ITG constraints. The checking algorithm for IST-ITG constraints is as follows.

1. For old translation candidates, the smallest **TRANSLATING** sub-tree t and its untranslated part u are calculated.
2. When a new target phrase f_{ph} is generated, the source phrase e_{ph} and untranslated part u calculated in above step are compared. If e_{ph} does not include and is not included in u, the new candidate is rejected. For example, in Figure 1, only source word e_a is already translated. The smallest **TRANSLATING** sub-tree is 1 and its untranslated part u is $[e_b e_c]$. In this case, phrases containing $[e_b]$, $[e_c]$, or $[e_b e_c]$ are accepted since these are included in u. Phrases $[e_b e_c e_d]$ or $[e_b e_c e_d e_e]$ are also accepted since these include u.
3. If a new candidate includes **NG** sub-trees, this candidate is rejected.

5 Experiments

5.1 Evaluation Measures

We evaluated the proposed method using four evaluation measures, BLEU (Papineni et al., 2002), NIST (Doddington 2002), WER(word error rate), and PER(position independent word error rate). Before discussing the evaluation, the characteristics of each one are analyzed.

- BLEU: This evaluation measure takes into account middle range word order, but does not take into account global word order. When the translation result is $[w_1, w_2, ..., w_{j-1}, X, w_{j+1}, ..., w_n]$ for reference translation $[w_1, w_2, ..., w_n]$, both WER and BLEU scores will be high. For a translation result $[w_{j+1}, ..., w_n, X, w_1, w_2, ..., w_{j-1}]$, the BLEU score will be the same as the previous result since BLEU only takes into account 4grams. However, the WER score will be zero since global word positions are taken into account. Therefore, the effectiveness of the proposed method using BLEU is less than that of using WER.

- NIST: This evaluation measure only takes into account n-grams like BLEU. However, importance of higher order n-grams are less than BLEU. Therefore, the effectiveness of the proposed method using NIST will be less than that of using BLEU.

- WER: This evaluation measure takes into account not only local but also global word order, and is the most suitable for evaluating our method.

- PER: With this evaluation measure, we are almost incapable of considering word order. Therefore, our proposed method would seem to offer no improvement in this evaluation measure.

5.2 English and Japanese Patent Corpus Experiments

First, we conducted experiments on English and Japanese patent translations. Details of the experimental corpus are shown in Table 2. This corpus is created by automatic sentence alignment (Uchiyama 2003). The first nine hundred sentence pairs with the best alignment scores were used as the evaluation data (single reference) and the next thousand sentence pairs were used as the development data. This corpus is a subset of the training corpus that will be used in the NTCIR-7 Workshop patent translation track.

Table 2: E-J patent corpus

	# of sent.	Total words	# of entries
E/J Train	1.8M	60M/64M	188K/118K
E/J Dev	916	30K/32K	4,072/3,646
E/J Eval	899	29K/32K	3,967/3,682

5.2.1 English-to-Japanese Translation

The translation direction of the first experiment was English-to-Japanese (E-J). For phrase-based translation model training, we used the GIZA++ toolkit (Och et al., 2003). For language model training, the SRI language model tool kit (Stolcke 2002) was used. The language model type was word 5-gram smoothed by Kneser-Ney discounting (Kneser 1995). For tuning of decoder parameters, we conducted minimum error training (Och 2003) with respect to the BLEU score using 916 development sentence pairs. For extraction of source sentence tree structure, we used the Charniak parser (Charniak 2000). We used Chasen for segmentation of the Japanese. The numbers of entries in the language models were 0.1 M, 2.1 M, 4.3 M, 6.2 M, and 6.9 M for 1, 2, 3, 4, and 5grams respectively. The number of entries in the phrase-table was 76 M. For decoding, we used an in-house decoder that is a close relative to the Moses decoder. The performance of this decoder was configured to be the same as Moses. Another conditions are the same as the default conditions of Moses decoder.

In the previous work (Zens et al., 2003, 2004), an IBM constraints and an ITG constraints are compared. In these experiments, a lexical reordering model, the proposed IST-ITC, and combinations of these are added as comparison targets. The combination of constraints in these experiments is as follows.

1. Monotone: Monotone translation (no reordering).
2. No constraints: There were no constraints for word reordering. Any word order was allowed without penalty.
3. IBM: IBM constraints without distortion limit.
4. ITG: ITG constraints.
5. IBM+ITG: Both IBM and ITG constraints were used at the same time.
6. IBM+LR: Both IBM constraints and lexical reordering model.
7. IST: Only the proposed IST-ITC constraints.
8. IBM+IST: Both IBM and IST-ITC constraints.
9. IBM+LR+IST: IBM constraints, Lexical reordering model, and IST-ITG constraints were used at the same time.

Table 3 shows the following experimental results. In comparing the original ITG constraints (ITG) with the proposed IST-ITG (IST) method, the improvement in BLEU was 2.67 points, and in WER was 5.39%. WER had the largest improvement, next was BLEU. This particular improvement order was the same as in the previous subsection. The large improvement of WER helped us confirm the effectiveness of the proposed method for global word ordering. When IBM constraints were used at the same time (IBM+ITG and IBM+IST), the BLEU score improved by 1.57 points and WER improved by 4.63%. When the lexical reordering model was used at the same time (IBM+LR and IBM+LR+IST), BLEU improved by 1.03 points and WER improved by 5.12%. The lexical reordering model fixed phrase position for the monotone and swap categories, but did not fix phrase position for the discontinuous category. IST-ITG fixed phrase position for the discontinuous category, even though it did not assign a probability. Combinations of the lexical reordering model and IST-ITG resulted in a better WER than with both IBM+LR and IBM+IST since both position and probability could be assigned for the discontinuous category.

Table 3: Evaluation results in E-J patent translation

	BLEU	NIST	WER	PER
Monotone	24.91	6.95	79.97	42.02
No constraint	26.83	7.19	81.10	39.52
IBM	28.35	7.29	78.35	39.25
ITG	27.59	7.26	80.29	39.15
IBM+ITG	28.50	7.30	78.01	39.29
IBM+LR	31.17	7.50	76.30	38.61
IST	30.26	7.41	74.90	38.93
IBM+IST	30.07	7.41	73.38	39.05
IBM+LR+IST	32.20	7.61	71.18	38.15

5.2.2 Japanese-to-English Translation

Next, we conducted J-E translation experiments using the same corpus. The numbers of entries in the language models were 0.2 M, 3.1 M, 4.1 M, 5.7 M, and 5.9 M for 1, 2, 3, 4, and 5grams The improvement. The number of entries in the phrase-table was 76 M. For parsing of Japanese, we used the dependency structure analyzer CaboCha. From the dependency structure, Japanese bracketed trees were generated. The combination of constraints in these experiments was the same as those of the E-J translation experiments.

Table 4 shows the translation results of sentence evaluation with the top five alignment scores. In comparing the original ITG constraints (ITG) with the proposed IST-ITG (IST), BLEU was improved by 1.21 points, and by in 3.81% in WER. The largest improvement was in WER, and BLEU had the next largest. This particular improvement order of these evaluation measures was the same as that of the E-J translation experiments. When IBM constraints were used at the same time (IBM+ITG and IBM+IST), there was no improvement in BLEU, but WER improved by 3.89%. When the lexical reordering model was used at the same time (IBM+LR and IBM+LR+IST), there was also no improvement in BLEU, but WER improved by 4.47%. One possible reason for the small (or no) improvement in BLEU is the lower parsing accuracy of Japanese compared with that of the English. However, better the WER figure indicates that using IST-ITC constraints leads to better word order. In the Appendix, differences in the translation results for the first five evaluation sentences between IBM+LR (Baseline:) and IBM+LR+IST (Proposed:) are shown.

Table 4: Evaluation results in J-E patent translation

	BLEU	NIST	WER	PER
Monotone	26.29	7.25	76.42	40.85
No constraint	26.20	7.18	81.41	40.76
IBM	27.87	7.34	78.16	39.94
ITG	27.01	7.24	80.43	40.50
IBM+ITG	28.16	7.35	78.04	40.07
IBM+LR	29.93	7.54	77.27	39.12
IST	28.32	7.31	76.62	40.67
IBM+IST	28.14	7.32	74.13	40.40
IBM+LR+IST	29.77	7.50	72.80	39.73

5.3 NIST MT08 English-to-Chinese Translation Experiments

Next, we conducted English-to-Chinese (E-C) newspaper translation experiments for different language pairs. The training and evaluation corpora were used in the NIST MT08 evaluation campaign English-to-Chinese translation track. For the translation model training, we used 6.2M bilingual sentences. For the language model training, we used 20.1M sentences. A development set with 1,664 sentences was used as evaluation data in the Chinese-to-English translation track in the NIST MT07 evaluation campaign. A single reference was used in the development set. The evaluation set with 1,859 sentences is the same as MT08's evaluation data, with 4 references. Model training and decoding conditions were the same as those in the E-J experiments. In both baseline and proposed condition, IBM constraints and lexical reordering model were used at the same time. Therefore, the baseline conditions correspond to the IBM+LR condition in the J-E experiments, the proposed conditions correspond to the IBM+LR+IST in the J-E experiments.

The evaluation unit was both the Chinese character and word as defined by the PKU corpus. As in the E-J experiments, the improvements in WER and CER (character error rate) were large. The improvements in WER, CER, word BLEU, and character BLEU were 5.3% (from 75.0% to 69.7%), 6.2% (from 74.1% to 67.9%), 2.2-points (from 21.0 to 23.2), and 1.8-points (from 35.2 to 37.0) respectively. We again demonstrated that the proposed method is effective (especially in WER) for multiple language pairs.

6 Conclusion

We proposed new word reordering constraints for PBSMT using source tree structure. The proposed IST-ITG constraints are extensions of the ITG constraints. In ITG constraints, the instance of the source-side tree is not taken into account. On the other hand, in IST-ITG constraints, the tree that is obtained by source sentence parsing is imposed on the decoding process. Therefore, IST-ITG constraints are stronger than those of the original ITG. For example, for four-word source sentences, IST-ITG constraints allow eight word orderings in a target sentence compared with twenty-two orderings under the original ITG constraints. IST-ITG constraints can be applied to a common decoder to determine a target sentence from one-pass without rescoring. In our E-J patent translation experiments, the proposed method resulted in a 2.7-point improvement in BLEU and a 5.7% improvement in WER compared with those of the original ITG constraints. In this paper we have argued the WER is the most appropriate measure to gauge the effectiveness of our approach since it gives importance to the global word order. Our approach gave rise to considerable gains in term of WER in all of our experiments, indicating that a respectable improvement in global word order was achieved. The improvement could clearly be seen from visual inspection of the output, a few examples of which are presented in the following Appendix.

A Samples from the Translation of Japanese Patent into English

A.1 Sentence 1

Source: そして、ロータ１６とステータ１５との間に充填した液体の運動エネルギーが熱エネルギーに変換されて制動トルクを発生する。
Reference: and, the kinetic energy of the liquid filled between the rotor 16 and stator 15 is converted into thermal energy to thereby produce a brake torque.
Baseline: then, the rotor 16 and the kinetic energy is converted to thermal energy braking torque is gener-

ated between the liquid filled in the stator 15.
Proposed: then, the rotor 16 and between the stator 15, the liquid filling the kinetic energy is converted to thermal energy braking torque is generated.

A.2 Sentence 2

Source: 7はシール材であり、後述の加工ガス9のシールと移動ホルダ3のガイドを兼ねたものである。
Reference: a sealant 7, which serves as a seal for cutting gas 9, also serves as a guide for the moving holder 3.
Baseline: the seal and movement of the holder 3 also serves as a guide for the seal member 7 is a work gas 9.
Proposed: 7 denotes a seal material, which also serves as a guide for the working gas 9 described later seal and movement of the holder 3.

A.3 Sentence 3

Source: 次に、車両前方の交差点の信号機が赤であり、運転者は信号機が赤であることを認知しており、停止しようとして、アクセルからブレーキに踏み換えようとしている場合を例として説明する。
Reference: suppose that the red signal light of a traffic signal installed at a crossing situated ahead is on, the driver has recognized the red signal light, and the driver 's foot is about to shift from the accelerator pedal to the brake pedal to stop the vehicle.
Baseline: next , the tread brake by the driver, the accelerator to be stopped from the traffic of recognizing traffic signals is " red " and the intersection ahead of the vehicle is red, it is described as an example.
Proposed: next, a case will be exemplified below so as to tread brakes from the accelerator to be stopped, and of recognizing traffic signals of red, the driver is " red " and is traffic light ahead of the vehicle.

A.4 Sentence 4

Source: さらに、被塗装物の表面を予め洗浄し、塗膜が付着しやすいように前処理、乾燥等の工程を必要とし、経済的でない。
Reference: in addition, this method is not economical because it requires special steps such as prewashing of the substrate surface, pre-treatments for providing the substrate with adherability to a coating, a drying step and the like.
Baseline: further, the coating film is apt to be deposited on the surface of the object to be coated by washing and drying process is required, and the preliminary process advance not economical.
Proposed: further, to clean the surface of the object to be coated beforehand so as to facilitate the adhesion of the coating film preprocessing and drying process is required, and not economical.

A.5 Sentence 5

Source: 4は送油路を示し、本体1の中空部をもって構成してある。
Reference: an oil passage 4 is formed as a hollow portion in the main body 1.
Baseline: 4 is a hollow portion of the body 1 with an oil supply passage is shown.
Proposed: 4 is an oil supply passage, with a hollow portion of the main body 1.

References

Adam L. Berger, Peter F. Brown, Stephen A. Della Pietra, Vincent J. Della Pietra, Andrew S. Kehler, and Robert L. Mercer, "Language translation apparatus and method of using context-based translation models, "United States patent, patent number 5510981, April, 1996.

Cabocha
http://chasen.org/ taku/software/cabocha/

Eugene Charniak, "A Maximum-Entropy-Inspired Parser," Proc. NAACL-2000, Seattle, Washington, pp.132-139, 2000.

Chasen
http://chasen-legacy.sourceforge.jp/

Yuan Ding, Martha Palmer, "Machine translation using probabilistic synchronous dependency insert grammars," Proc. ACL, Ann Arbor, pp. 541-548, 2005.

George Doddington, "Automatic evaluation of machine translation quality using n-gram co-occurrence statistics," Proc. ARPA Workshop on Human Language Technology, San Diego, CA, 2002.

Michel Galley, Jonathan Graehl, Kevin Knight, Daniel Marcu, Steve DeNeefe, Wei Wang, Ignacio Thayer, "Scalable Inference and Training of Context-Rich Syntactic Models,"Proc. ACL-COLING, Sydney Australia, pp. 961-968, 2006.

Liang Huang, Kevin Knight, Aravind Joshi, "Statistical Syntax-Directed Translation with Extended Domain of Locality," Proc. AMTA, Massachusetts, 2006

Reinhard Kneser, Hermann Ney, "Improved backing-off for m-gram language model," Proceedings of the IEEE International Conference of Acoustic, Speech, and Signal processing. Vol. 1, pp. 181-184, 1995.

Yang Liu, Qun Liu, Shouxun Lin, "Tree-to-String Alignment Template for Statistical Machine Translation," Proc. ACL-COLING, Sydney Australia, pp. 609-616, 2006.

Daniel Marcu, William Wong, "A phrase-based, joint probability model for statistical machine translation," Proc. EMNLP-2002, Philadelphia, pp.133-139, 2002. p. 127-133, 2003.

Daniel Marcu, Wei Wang, Abdessamad Echihabi, Kevin Knight, "SPMT: Statistical Machine Translation with Syntactifi ed Target Language Phrases,"Proc. EMNLP-2006, Sydney Australia, pp. 44-52, 2006.

Dan Melamed, "Statistical machine translation by parsing, "Proc. ACL, Barcelona, pp. 653-660, 2004.

Moses
http://www.statmt.org/moses/

NIST MT08
http://www.nist.gov/speech/tests/mt/2008/

NTCIR-7
http://ntcir.nii.ac.jp/

Franz Josef Och, Hermann Ney, "A Systematic Comparison of Various Statistical Alignment Models," Computational Linguistics, No. 1, Vol. 29, pp. 19-51, 2003.

Franz Josef Och, "Minimum error rate training for statistical machine trainslation,"Proc. ACL, Sapporo Japan, pp. 160-167, 2003.

Franz Josef Och, Hermann Ney, "The alignment template approach to statistical machine translation, Computational Linguistics, 30(4), pp417-449, 2004.

Kishore Papineni, Salim Roukos, Todd Ward, Wei-Jing Zhu, "Bleu: a method for automatic evaluation of machine translation," Proc. ACL, Philadelphia PA, pp. 311-318, 2002.

Chris Quirk, Arul Menezes, Colin Cherry, "Dependency treelet translation: Syntactically informed phrasal SMT," Proc. ACL, Ann Arbor, pp. 271-279, 2005.

Andreas Stolcke, "SRILM - An Extensible Language Model Toolkit,"Proc. ICSLP'02, Denver, pp. 901-904, 2002. http://www.speech.sri.com/projects/srilm/

Christopher Tillmann, "A unigram orientation model for statistical machine translation,"HLT-NAACL, Boston, pp. 101-104, 2004.

Masao Uchiyama and Hitoshi Isahara, "Reliable Measures for Aligning Japanese-English News Articles and Sentences", Proc. ACL, Sapporo Japan, pp. 72-79, 2003.

Dekai Wu, "Stochastic inversion transduction grammars, with application to segmentation, bracketing, and alignment of parallel corpora," In Proc. IJCAI, pp. 1328-1334, Montreal, 1995.

Dekai Wu, "Stochastic inversion transuduction grammars and bilingual parsing of parallel corpora," Computational Linguiatics, 23(3), pp.377-403, 1997.

Kenji Yamada, Kevin Knight, "A syntax-based statistical translation model," Proc. ACL, Hong Kong, pp. 523-530, 2000.

Richard Zens, Hermann Ney, "A Comparative Study on Reordering Constraints in Statistical Machine Translation" Proc. ACL, Sapporo Japan, pp. 144-151, 2003.

Richard Zens, Hermann Ney, Taro Watanabe, Eiichiro Sumita, "Reordering Constraints for Phrase-Based Statistical Machine Translation" Proc. Coling, Geneva, pp. 205-211, 2004.

A Scalable Decoder for Parsing-based Machine Translation with Equivalent Language Model State Maintenance

Zhifei Li and **Sanjeev Khudanpur**
Department of Computer Science and Center for Language and Speech Processing
Johns Hopkins University, Baltimore, MD 21218, USA
zhifei.work@gmail.com and khudanpur@jhu.edu

Abstract

We describe a scalable decoder for parsing-based machine translation. The decoder is written in JAVA and implements all the essential algorithms described in Chiang (2007): chart-parsing, m-gram language model integration, beam- and cube-pruning, and unique k-best extraction. Additionally, parallel and distributed computing techniques are exploited to make it scalable. We also propose an algorithm to maintain equivalent language model states that exploits the *back-off* property of m-gram language models: instead of maintaining a separate state for each distinguished sequence of "state" words, we merge multiple states that can be made *equivalent* for language model probability calculations due to back-off. We demonstrate experimentally that our decoder is more than 30 times faster than a baseline decoder written in PYTHON. We propose to release our decoder as an open-source toolkit.

1 Introduction

Large-scale parsing-based statistical machine translation (MT) has made remarkable progress in the last few years. The systems being developed differ in whether they use source- or target-language syntax. For instance, the hierarchical translation system of Chiang (2007) extracts a synchronous grammar from pairs of strings, Quirk et al. (2005), Liu et al. (2006) and Huang et al. (2006) perform syntactic analyses in the source-language, and Galley et al. (2006) use target-language syntax.

A critical component in parsing-based MT systems is the decoder, which is complex to implement and scale up. Most of the systems described above employ tailor-made, dedicated decoders that are not open-source, which results in a high barrier to entry for other researchers in the field. However, with the algorithms proposed in (Huang and Chiang, 2005; Chiang, 2007; Huang and Chiang, 2007), it is possible to develop a general-purpose decoder that can be used by all the parsing-based systems. In this paper, we describe an important first-step towards an extensible, general-purpose, scalable, and open-source parsing-based MT decoder. Our decoder is written in JAVA and implements all the essential algorithms described in Chiang (2007): chart-parsing, m-gram language model integration, beam- and cube-pruning, and unique k-best extraction. Additionally, parallel and distributed computing techniques are exploited to make it scalable.

Straightforward integration of an m-gram language model (LM) into a parsing-based decoder substantially increases its computational complexity. Therefore, it is important to develop efficient methods for LM integration. We propose an algorithm to maintain equivalent LM states by exploiting the *back-off* property of m-gram LMs. Specifically, instead of maintaining a separate state for each distinguished sequence of "state" words, we merge multiple states that can be made *equivalent* for LM calculations by anticipating such back-off.

We demonstrate experimentally that our decoder is 38 times faster than a previous decoder written in PYTHON. Furthermore, the distributed computing permits improving translation quality via large-scale LMs. We have successfully use our decoder to translate about a million sentences in a parallel corpus for large-scale discriminative training experiments.

Proceedings of the Second ACL Workshop on Syntax and Structure in Statistical Translation (SSST-2), pages 10–18,
ACL-08: HLT, Columbus, Ohio, USA, June 2008.

2 Parsing-based MT Decoder

In this section, we discuss the core algorithms implemented in our decoder. These algorithms have been discussed by Chiang (2007) in detail, and we recapitulate the essential parts here for completeness.

2.1 Grammar Formalism

Our decoder assumes a probabilistic synchronous context-free grammar (SCFG). Following the notation in Venugopal et al. (2007), a probabilistic SCFG comprises a set of source-language terminal symbols T_S, a set of target-language terminal symbols T_T, a shared set of nonterminal symbols N, and a set of rules of the form

$$X \rightarrow \langle \gamma, \alpha, \sim, w \rangle \,, \tag{1}$$

where $X \in N$, $\gamma \in [N \cup T_S]^*$ is a (mixed) sequence of nonterminals and source terminals, $\alpha \in [N \cup T_T]^*$ is a sequence of nonterminals and target terminals, $\sim$ is a one-to-one correspondence or *alignment* between the nonterminal elements of γ and α, and $w \geq 0$ is a weight assigned to the rule. An illustrative rule for Chinese-to-English translation is

$$NP \;\; \rightarrow \;\; \langle\, NP_0 \text{ 的 } NP_1 \,,\, NP_1 \text{ of } NP_0 \,\rangle \,,$$

where the Chinese word 的 (pronounced *de* or *di*) means *of*, and the alignment, encoded via subscripts on the nonterminals, causes the two noun phrases around 的 to be reordered around *of* in the translation. The rule weight is omitted in this example.

A bilingual SCFG derivation is analogous to a monolingual CFG derivation. It begins with a pair of *aligned* start symbols. At each step, an *aligned* pair of nonterminals is rewritten as the two corresponding components of a single rule. In this sense, the derivations are generated synchronously.

Our decoder presently handles SCFGs of the kind extracted by Heiro (Chiang, 2007), but is easily extensible to more general SCFGs and closely related formalisms such as synchronous tree substitution grammars (Eisner, 2003; Chiang, 2006).

2.2 MT Decoding as Chart Parsing

Given a source-language sentence f^*, the decoder must find the target-language yield $e(D)$ of the best derivation D among all derivations with source-language yield $f(D) = f^*$, i.e.

$$e^* \;=\; e\left(\arg \max_{D\,:\,f(D)=f^*} w(D)\right) \,, \tag{2}$$

where $w(D)$ is the composite weight of D.

The parser may be treated as a deductive proof system (Shieber et al., 1995). Formally (cf. (Chiang, 2007)), a parser defines a space of weighted *items*, with some items designated as *axioms* and some as *goals*, and a set of *inference rules* of the form

$$\frac{I_1 : w_1 \quad \cdots \quad I_k : w_k}{I : w} \quad \phi \,,$$

which states that if all the *antecedent* items I_i are provable, respectively with weight w_i, then the *consequent* item I is provable with weight w, provided the side condition ϕ holds. For a grammar with a maximum of two (pairs of) nonterminals per rule[1], Figure 1 illustrates the resulting chart parsing procedure, including the integration of an m-gram LM.

The actual decoding algorithm maintains a *chart*, which contains an array of *cells*. Each cell in turn maintains a list of proved *items*. The parsing process starts with the axioms, and proceeds by applying the inference rules to prove more and more items until a goal item is proved. Whenever the parser proves a new item, it adds the item to the appropriate chart cell. It also maintains backpointers to antecedent items, which are used for k-best extraction, as discussed in Section 2.4 below.

In a SCFG-based decoder, an *item* is identified by its source-language span, left-side nonterminal label, and left- and right-context for the target-language m-gram LM. Therefore, in a given *cell*, the maximum possible number of items is $O(|N||T_T|^{2(m-1)})$, and the worst case decoding complexity is

$$O\left(|N|^K \, |T_T|^{2K(m-1)} n^3\right) \,, \tag{3}$$

where K is the maximum number of nonterminal pairs per rule and n is the source-language sentence length (Venugopal et al., 2007).

[1]For more general grammars with $K \geq 2$ pairs of nonterminals per rule, see Venugopal et al. (2007).

$$\frac{}{X \to \langle \gamma, \alpha \rangle : w} \quad (X \to \langle \gamma, \alpha, w \rangle) \in G$$

$$\frac{X \to \langle f_{i+1}^{j}, \alpha \rangle : w}{[X, i, j; q(\alpha)] : wp(\alpha)}$$

$$\frac{Z \to \langle f_{i+1}^{i_1} X f_{j_1+1}^{j}, \alpha \rangle : w \quad [X, i_1, j_1; e_1] : w_1}{[Z, i, j; q(\alpha')] : ww_1 p(\alpha')} \quad \alpha' = \alpha[e_1/X]$$

$$\frac{Z \to \langle f_{i+1}^{i_1} X_1 f_{j_1+1}^{i_2} Y_2 f_{j_2+1}^{j}, \alpha \rangle : w \quad [X, i_1, j_1; e_1] : w_1 \quad [Y, i_2, j_2; e_2] : w_2}{[Z, i, j; q(\alpha')] : ww_1 w_2 p(\alpha')} \quad \alpha' = \alpha[e_1/X_1, e_2/Y_2]$$

$$\text{Goal item: } [S, 0, n; \langle s \rangle^{m-1} \star e \langle /s \rangle]$$

Figure 1: Inference rules from Chiang (2007) for a parser with an m-gram LM. G denotes the translation grammar. $w[x/X]$ denotes substitution of the string x for the symbol X in the string w. The function $p(\cdot)$ provides the LM probability for all *complete* m-grams in a string, while the function $q(\cdot)$ elides symbols whose m-grams have been accounted for by $p(\cdot)$. Details about the functions $p(\cdot)$ and $q(\cdot)$ are provided in Section 4.

2.3 Pruning in a Decoder

Severe pruning is needed in order to make the decoding computationally feasible for SCFGs with large vocabularies T_T and detailed nonterminal sets. In our decoder, we incorporate two pruning techniques described by (Chiang, 2007; Huang and Chiang, 2007). For *beam pruning*, in each cell, we discard all items whose weight is worse, by a relative threshold β, than the weight of the best item in the same cell. If too many items pass the threshold, a cell only retains the top-b items by weight. When combining smaller items to obtain a larger item by applying an inference rule, we use *cube-pruning* to simulate k-best extraction in each destination cell, and discard combinations that lead to an item whose weight is worse than the best item in that cell by a margin of ϵ.

2.4 k-best Extraction Over Hyper-graphs

For each source-language sentence f^*, the output of the chart-parsing algorithm may be treated as a *hyper-graph* representing a set of likely hypotheses D in (2). Briefly, a hyper-graph is a set of *vertices* and *hyper-edges*, with each hyper-edge connecting a *set* of antecedent vertices to a consequent vertex, and a special vertex designated as the *target vertex*. In parsing parlance, a vertex corresponds to an item in the chart, a hyper-edge corresponds to a SCFG rule with the nonterminals on the right-side replaced by back-pointers to antecedent items, and the target vertex corresponds to the goal item[2].

Given a hyper-graph for a source-language sentence f^*, we use the k-best extraction algorithm of Huang and Chiang (2005) to extract its k most likely translations. Moreover, since many different derivations D in (2) may lead to the same target-language yield $e(D)$, we adopt the modification described in Huang et al. (2006) to efficiently generate the *unique* k best translations of f^*.

3 Parallel and Distributed Computing

Many applications of parsing-based MT entail the use of SCFGs extracted from millions of bilingual sentence pairs and LMs extracted from billions of words of target-language text. This requires the decoder to make use of *distributed* computing to spread the memory required to load large-scale SCFGs and LMs onto *multiple processors*. Furthermore, techniques such as iterative minimum errorrate training (Och et al., 2003) as well as web-based MT services require the decoder to translate a large number of source-language sentences per unit time. This requires the decoder to make use of *parallel* computing to utilize each *individual multi-core processor* more effectively. We have incorporated two such performance enhancements in our decoder.

[2] In a decoder integrating an m-gram LM, there may be multiple goal items due to different LM contexts. However, one can image a *single* goal item identified by the span $[0, n]$ and the goal nonterminal S, but not by the LM contexts.

3.1 Parallel Decoding

We have enhanced our decoder to translate multiple source-language sentences in parallel by exploiting the ability of a multi-core processor to concurrently run several *threads* that share memory. Specifically, given one (or more) document(s) containing multiple source-language sentences, the decoder automatically splits the set of sentences into several subsets, and initiates concurrent decoding threads; once all the threads finish, the main thread merges back the translations. Since all the threads naturally share memory, the decoder needs to load the (large) SCFG and LM into memory *only once*. This multithreading provides a very significant speed-up.

3.2 Distributed Language Models

It is not possible in some cases to load a very large LM into memory on a *single* machine, particularly if the SCFG is also very large. In other cases, loading the LM each time the decoder runs may be too time-consuming relative to the time required for decoding itself, such as in iterative decoding with updated combination weights during minimum error-rate training. It is therefore desirable to have dedicated servers to load parts of the LM[3] — an idea that has been exploited by (Zhang et al., 2006; Emami et al., 2007; Brants et al., 2007).

Our implementation can load a (partitioned) LM on different servers before initiating decoding. The decoder remotely calls the servers to obtain individual LM probabilities, and linearly interpolates them on the fly using a given set of interpolation weights. With this architecture, one can deal with a very large target-language text corpus by splitting it into many parts and training separate LMs from each. The run-time interpolation capability may also be used for LM adaptation, e.g. for building document-specific language models.

To mitigate potential network communication delays inherent to a distributed LM, we implement a simple *cache* mechanism in the *decoder*. The cache saves the outcomes of the most recent LM calls, including interpolated LM probabilities; the cache is reset whenever its size exceeds a threshold. We could have maintained a cache at each *LM server* as well; however, the resultant saving is not significant because the *trie* data-structures used to implement m-gram LMs are quite fast relative to the cache lookup overhead.

[3]Similarly, distributing the SCFG is also possible.

4 Equivalent LM-state Maintenance

It is clear from the complexity (3) of the inference rules (Figure 1) that a straightforward integration of an m-gram LM adds a multiplicative factor of $|T_T|^{2K(m-1)}$ to the computational complexity of the decoder, where T_T is the set of target-language terminal symbols. We illustrate in this section how this potentially very large multiplier can be dramatically reduced by exploiting the *structure* of the LM.

4.1 Applying an m-gram LM in the Decoder

Integrating an LM into chart parsing requires two functions $p(\cdot)$ and $q(\cdot)$ (see Figure 1) that operate on strings over $T_T \cup \{\star\}$, where $\star$ is a special "placeholder" symbol for an elided part of a target-language string.

The function $p(e)$ calculates the LM probability of the *complete* m-grams in $e \equiv e_1 \ldots e_l$, i.e.

$$p(e_1 \ldots e_l) \;=\; \prod_{m \le i \le l \;\&\; \star \notin e^{i}_{i-(m-1)}} P_{\mathrm{LM}}(e_i \,|\, h_i)\,, \quad (4)$$

where $h_i = e_{i-(m-1)} \cdots e_{i-1}$ is the $m-1$-word "LM history" of the target-language word e_i.

Since the p-probability of e does not include the LM probability for the *partial* m-grams (i.e., the first $(m-1)$ words) of e, the *exact* weights of two items $[X, i, j; e]$ and $[X, i, j; e']$ in the chart are *not* available during the bottom-up pruning of Section 2.3. Therefore, as an approximation, we also compute

$$\hat{p}(e) \;=\; \prod_{k=1}^{\min\{m-1, |e|\}} P_{\mathrm{LM}}(e_k \,|\, e_1 \ldots e_{k-1}), \quad (5)$$

an *estimate* of the LM probability of the $m-1$-gram prefix of e. This estimated probability is taken into account for pruning purposes (only).

The function $q(e_1 \ldots e_l)$ determines the left and right *LM states* that must be maintained for future computation of the *exact* LM probability, respectively, of $e_1 \ldots e_{m-1}$ and $e_{l+1} \ldots e_{l+m-1}$.

$$q(e_1 \ldots e_l) \quad (6)$$

$$= \begin{cases} e_1 \ldots e_l & \text{if } l < m-1, \\ e_1 \ldots e_{m-1} \star e_{l-(m-2)} \cdots e_l & \text{otherwise.} \end{cases}$$

4.2 Back-off Parameterization of m-gram LMs

While many different methods are popular for estimating m-gram LMs, most store the estimated LM parameters in the ARPA *back-off* file format; using the notation e_i^j to denote a target-language word sequence $e_i\, e_{i+1}\, \ldots\, e_j$, the LM probability calculation is carried out as

$$P_{\mathrm{BO}}(e_m \mid e_1^{m-1}) \tag{7}$$

$$= \begin{cases} \pi(e_1^m) & \text{if } e_1^m \in \text{LM} \\ \beta(e_1^{m-1}) \times P_{\mathrm{BO}}(e_m \mid e_2^{m-1}) & \text{otherwise,} \end{cases}$$

where the *lower order* probability $P_{\mathrm{BO}}(e_m \mid e_2^{m-1})$ is recursively defined in the same way, and $\beta(e_1^{m-1})$ is the back-off weight of the history. The LM file contains the parameter $\pi(\cdot)$ for each *listed* m-gram, and the parameters $\pi(\cdot)$ and $\beta(\cdot)$ for each listed $\widetilde{m}$-gram, $1 \leq \widetilde{m} < m$; for *unlisted* $\widetilde{m}$-grams, $\beta(\cdot) = 1$ by definition.

Observe from (7) that if e_1^m is *not listed* in the LM, the back-off weight $\beta(\cdot)$ is the same for all words e_m, and the backed-off probability $P_{\mathrm{BO}}(e_m \mid \cdot)$ is the same for all words e_1. Furthermore, as m grows, the fraction of possible m-grams actually observed in a training corpus diminishes rapidly.

4.3 The Equivalent LM State of an Item

The maximum possible number of items in a *cell* increases exponentially with the LM order m, as discussed in Section 2.2. With pruning (cf. Section 2.3), we restrict the maximum number of items in each cell to some threshold b. Intuitively, therefore, if we increase the LM order m, we should also increase the beam size b to reduce search errors. This could slow down the decoder significantly.

Recall from the previous subsection, however, that when m increases, the fraction of m-grams that will need to back-off also increases. Moreover, even for modest values of m, the decoder considers many "unseen" m-grams (due to reordering and translation combinations) that do not appear in natural texts, leading to frequent back-off during the LM probability calculation (7). In this subsection, we propose a method to collapse equivalent LM states so that the decoder effectively considers many more items in each cell without increasing beam size.

We merge multiple LM states (6) that already have—or back-off to—the *same* "LM history" in the calculation (7) of LM probabilities, e.g. due to different unlisted m-grams that back-off to the same $m-1$-gram. For simplicity, we only consider LM state merging by the function $q(\cdot)$ of (6) when $l \geq m-1$.

Though the equivalent LM state maintenance technique is discussed here in the context of a parsing-based MT decoder, it is also applicable to standard left-to-right phrase-based decoders. In particular, the right-side equivalent LM state maintenance proposed in Section 4.3.1 may be used.

4.3.1 Obtaining the Equivalent Right LM State

Recall that the *right* LM state $e_{l-(m-2)}^{l}$ of e_1^l serves as the "LM history" for calculating the *exact* LM probabilities of the yet-to-be-determined word e_{l+1}. Recall further the computation (7) of $P_{\mathrm{BO}}(e_{l+1} \mid e_{l-(m-2)}^{l})$.

- If the m-gram $e_{l-(m-2)}^{l+1}$ is *not listed* in the LM for *any* word e_{l+1}, then the LM will back-off to $P_{\mathrm{BO}}(e_{l+1} \mid e_{l-(m-3)}^{l})$, which does not depend on the word $e_{l-(m-2)}$.
- If the $m-1$-gram $e_{l-(m-2)}^{l}$ also is not listed in the LM, then $\beta(e_{l-(m-2)}^{l}) = 1$.

If these two conditions hold true, $q(\cdot)$ may safely elide the word $e_{l-(m-2)}$ in (6) no matter what words follow e_1^l. The *right* LM state is thus reduced from $m-1$ words to $m-2$ words.

The argument above can be applied recursively to the resulting right LM state $e_{l-(m-2)+i}^{l}$, where $i \in [0, m-2]$, leading to the *equivalent right state* computation procedure of Figure 2. The procedure IS-A-PREFIX($e_1^{\widetilde{m}}$) checks if its argument $e_1^{\widetilde{m}}$ is a prefix of any k-gram listed in the LM, $k \in [\widetilde{m}, m]$.

4.3.2 Obtaining the Equivalent Left LM State

Recall that the *left* LM state e_1^{m-1} of e_1^l is the prefix whose exact LM probability is unknown during bottom-up parsing, and is replaced by the estimated probability $\hat{p}(e_1^{m-1})$ of (5) for pruning purposes. Recall further the computation (7) of $P_{\mathrm{BO}}(e_{m-1} \mid e_0^{m-2})$.

- If the m-gram e_0^{m-1} is *not listed* in the LM for *any* word e_0, then it will back-off to

EQ-R-STATE $(e_{l-(m-2)}^{l})$

for $i \leftarrow 0$ **to** $m-2$ ▷ left to right
  if IS-A-PREFIX $(e_{l-(m-2)+i}^{l})$
    break ▷ stop reducing `ers`
  else
    `ers` $\leftarrow e_{l-(m-2)+i+1}^{l}$ ▷ reduce state
return `ers`

Figure 2: Equivalent Right LM State Computation.

> $P_{\text{BO}}(e_{m-1} \mid e_1^{m-2})$, which can be computed right away based on e_1^{m-1} without waiting for the unknown e_0. Moreover, the back-off weight $\beta(e_0^{m-2})$ does not depend on the word e_{m-1}.

Therefore, $q(\cdot)$ may safely elide the word e_{m-1}, and reduce the *left* LM state in (6) from e_1^{m-1} to e_1^{m-2}. Also, $p(\cdot)$ should also co-opt $P_{\text{BO}}(e_{m-1} \mid e_1^{m-2})$ into the *complete* m-gram probability of (4) and $\hat{p}(\cdot)$ should exclude e_{m-1} in (5).

The argument above can again be applied recursively to the resulting left LM state e_1^i, $i \in [1, m-1]$, leading to the *equivalent left state* procedure of Figure 3. The procedure IS-A-SUFFIX($e_1^{\widetilde{m}}$) checks if $e_1^{\widetilde{m}}$ is a suffix of any listed k-gram in the LM, $k \in [\widetilde{m}, m]$. In Figure 3, `fin` refers to the probability that can be computed right away based on the state itself, for co-opting into the *complete* m-gram probability of (4) as mentioned above.

4.3.3 Modified Cost Functions for Parsing

When carrying out the reduction of the left and right LM states to their shortest equivalents, the formula (4) for calculating the probability of the *complete* m-grams in an item $[X, i, j; e]$, where $e = e_1^l$, is modified as

$$p(e_1^l) = \text{EQ-L-STATE}(e_1^{m-1}).\texttt{fin} \times \prod_{m \le i \le l \,\&\, \star \notin e_{i-(m-1)}^{i}} P_{\text{LM}}(e_i \mid h_i)$$

with the further qualification that some care must be taken later to incorporate the back-off weights of the "LM histories" of the suffix of e_1^{m-1} that went missing due to left LM state reduction.

EQ-L-STATE (e_1^{m-1})

`els` $\leftarrow e_1^{m-1}$
`fin` $\leftarrow 1$ ▷ update to final probability p
for $i \leftarrow m-1$ **to** 1 ▷ right to left
  if IS-A-SUFFIX(e_1^i)
    break ▷ stop reducing `els`
  else
    `fin` $\leftarrow P_{\text{BO}}(e_i \mid e_1^{i-1}) \times$ `fin`
    `els` $\leftarrow e_1^{i-1}$ ▷ reduce state
return `els`, `fin`

Figure 3: Equivalent Left LM State Computation.

The estimated probability of the left LM state is modified as

$$\hat{p}(e) = \begin{cases} \hat{p}(e) & \text{if } |e| < m-1 \\ \hat{p}(\text{EQ-L-STATE}(e_1^{m-1}).\texttt{els}) & \text{otherwise,} \end{cases}$$

with $\hat{p}$ as defined in (5).

Finally, the LM state function is

$$q(e_1^l) = \begin{cases} e_1 \ldots e_l & \text{if } l < m-1 \\ \text{EQ-L-STATE}(e_1^{m-1}).\texttt{els} \star & \\ \quad \text{EQ-R-STATE}(e_{l-(m-2)}^{l}).\texttt{ers} & \text{otherwise.} \end{cases}$$

4.3.4 Suffix and Prefix Look-Up

As done in the SRILM toolkit (Stolcke, 2002), a back-off m-gram LM is stored using a reverse *trie* data structure. We store the suffix and prefix information in the same data structure without incurring much additional memory cost. Specifically, the prefix information is stored at the back-off state, while the suffix information is stored as one bit alongside the regular m-gram probability.

5 Experimental Results

In this section, we evaluate the performance of our decoder on a Chinese to English translation task.

5.1 System Training

We use various parallel text corpora distributed by the Linguistic Data Consortium (LDC) for the NIST MT evaluation. The parallel data we select contains about 570K Chinese-English sentence pairs, adding up to about 19M words on each side. To train the English language models, we use the English side of the parallel text and a subset of the English Gigaword corpus, for a total of about 130M words.

We use the GIZA toolkit (Och and Ney, 2000), a suffix-array architecture (Lopez, 2007), the SRILM toolkit (Stolcke, 2002), and minimum error rate training (Och et al., 2003) to obtain word-alignments, a translation model, language models, and the optimal weights for combining these models, respectively.

5.2 Improvements in Decoding Speed

We use a PYTHON implementation of a state-of-the-art decoder as our baseline[4] for decoder comparisons. For a direct comparison, we use exactly the same models and pruning parameters. The SCFG contains about 3M rules, the 5-gram LM explicitly lists about 49M k-grams, $k = 1, 2, \ldots, 5$, and the pruning uses $\beta = 10$, $b = 30$ and $\epsilon = 0.1$.

Decoder	Speed (sec/sent)	BLEU-4	
		MT '03	MT '05
Python	26.5	34.4%	32.7%
Java	1.2	**34.5%**	**32.9%**
Java (parallel)	**0.7**		

Table 1: Decoder Comparison: Translation speed and quality on the 2003 and 2005 NIST MT benchmark tests.

As shown in Table 1, the JAVA decoder (without explicit parallelization) is 22 times *faster* than the PYTHON decoder, while achieving slightly *better* translation quality as measured by BLEU-4 (Papineni et al., 2002). The parallelization further speeds it up by a factor of 1.7, making the parallel JAVA decoder is 38 times faster than the PYTHON decoder.

We have used the decoder to successfully decode about one million sentences for a large-scale discriminative training experiment.

5.3 Impact of a Distributed Language Model

We use the SRILM toolkit to build eight 7-gram language models, and load and call the LMs using a distributed LM architecture[5] as discussed in Section 3.2. As shown in Table 2, the 7-gram distributed language model (DLM) significantly improves translation performance over the 5-gram LM. However, decoding is significantly slower (12.2 sec/sent when using the non-parallel decoder) due to the added network communication overhead.

LM type	# k-grams	MT '03	MT '05
5-gram LM	49 M	34.5%	32.9%
7-gram DLM	310 M	**35.5%**	**33.9%**

Table 2: Distributed language model: the 7-gram LM cannot be loaded alongside the SCFG on a single machine; via distributed computing, it yields significant improvement in BLEU-4 over a 5-gram.

5.4 Utility of Equivalent LM States

To reduce the number of search errors, one may either increase the beam size, or employ techniques such as the equivalent LM state maintenance described in Section 4. In this subsection, we compare the tradeoff between the search effort (measured by decoding time per sentence) and the search quality (measured by the average model cost of the best translation found).

Intuitively, collapsing equivalent LM states is useful only when the language model is very sparse, i.e., most of the evaluated m-grams will need to back-off. A sparse LM is obtained in practice by using a large order m relative to the amount of training data. To test this intuition, we train a 7-gram LM using *only* the English side of the parallel text ($\sim$ 19M words). Figure 4 compares maintenance of the full LM state v/s the equivalent LM state. The beam size b for decoding with equivalent LM states is fixed at 30; it is increased considerably—30, 50, 70, 90, 120, and 150—with the full LM state in an effort to reduce search errors. It is clear from the figure that collapsing items that differ due only to equivalent LM states improves the search quality considerably while actually reducing search effort. This shows the effectiveness of equivalent LM state maintenance.

[4] We are extremely thankful to Philip Resnik at University of Maryland for allowing us the use of their PYTHON decoder as the baseline. Thanks also go to David Chiang who originally implement the decoder.

[5] Since our distributed LM architecture dynamically interpolates multiple LM scores, it cannot yet exploit the equivalent LM state maintenance of Section 4, for different LMs will have different reduced LM states. We will address this in the future.

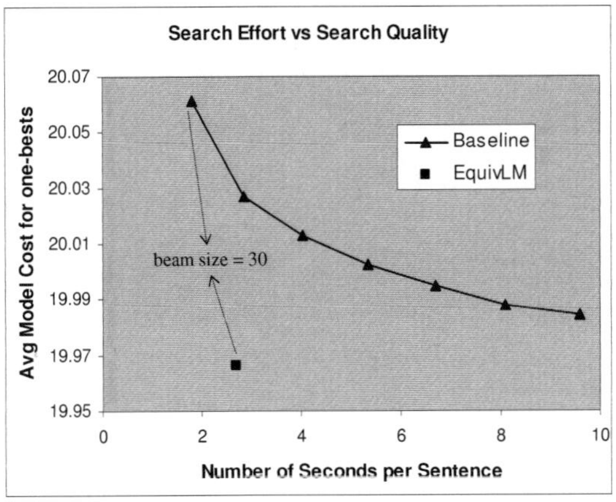

Figure 4: Search quality with equivalent 7-gram LM state maintenance (EquivLM) and without it (Baseline) as a function of search effort as controlled by the beam size.

We also train a 3-gram LM using an English corpus of about 130M words, and repeat the above experiments. In this case, maintaining equivalent LM states costs *more* decoding time than using the full LM state to achieve the same search quality. This is due partly to our inefficient implementation of the prefix- and suffix-lookup required to determine the equivalent LM state, and partly to the fact that with 130M words, a 3-gram LM backs off less frequently.

6 Conclusions

We have described a scalable decoder for parsing-based machine translation. It is written in JAVA and implements all the essential algorithms described in Chiang (2007): chart-parsing, m-gram language model integration, beam- and cube-pruning, and unique k-best extraction. Additionally, parallel and distributed computing techniques are exploited to make it scalable. We demonstrate that our decoder is 38 times faster than a baseline decoder written in PYTHON, and that the distributed language model is very useful to improve translation quality in a large-scale task. We also describe an algorithm that exploits the *back-off* property of an m-gram model to maintain equivalent LM states, and show that better search quality is obtained with less search effort when the search space is organized to exploit this equivalence. We plan to incorporate some additional syntax-based components into the decoder and release it as an open-source toolkit.

Acknowledgments

We thank Philip Resnik, Chris Dyer, Smaranda Muresan and Adam Lopez for very helpful discussions, and the anonymous reviewers for their constructive comments. This research was partially supported by the Defense Advanced Research Projects Agency's GALE program via Contract No HR0011-06-2-0001.

References

Thorsten Brants, Ashok C. Popat, Peng Xu, Franz J. Och, and Jeffrey Dean. 2006. Large Language Models in Machine Translation. *In Proceedings of EMNLP 2007.*

David Chiang. 2006. An Introduction to Synchronous Grammars. Available at http://www.isi.edu/~chiang/papers/synchtut.pdf.

David Chiang. 2007. Hierarchical phrase-based translation. *Computational Linguistics*, 33(2):201-228.

Jason Eisner. 2003. Learning non-isomorphic tree mappings for machine translation. *In Proceedings of ACL 2003.*

Ahmad Emami, Kishore Papineni, and Jeffrey Sorensen. 2007. Large-scale distributed language modeling. *In Proceedings of ICASSP 2007.*

Michel Galley, Jonathan Graehl, Kevin Knight, Daniel Marcu, Steve DeNeefe, Wei Wang, and Ignacio Thayer. 2006. Scalable inference and training of context-rich syntactic translation models. *In Proceedings of COLING/ACL 2006.*

Liang Huang and David Chiang. 2005. Better k-best parsing. *In Proceedings of IWPT 2005.*

Liang Huang and David Chiang. 2007. Forest Rescoring: Faster Decoding with Integrated Language Models. *In Proceedings of the ACL 2007.*

Liang Huang, Kevin Knight, and Aravind Joshi. 2006. Statistical syntax-directed translation with extended domain of locality. *In Proceedings of AMTA 2006.*

Yang Liu, Qun Liu, and Shouxun Lin. 2006. Tree-to-string alignment template for statistical machine translation. *In Proceedings of COLING-ACL 2006.*

Adam Lopez. 2007. Hierarchical Phrase-Based Translation with Suffix Arrays. *In Proceedings of EMNLP 2007.*

Franz Josef Och. 2003. Minimum error rate training in statistical machine translation. *In Proceedings of ACL 2003.*

Franz Josef Och and Hermann Ney. 2000. Improved statistical alignment models. *In Proceedings of ACL 2000.*

Kishore Papineni, Salim Roukos, Todd Ward, and Wei-Jing Zhu. 2002. BLEU: a method for automatic evaluation of machine translation. *In Proceedings of ACL 2002.*

Chris Quirk, Arul Menezes, and Colin Cherry. 2005. Dependency Treelet Translation: Syntactically Informed Phrasal SMT. *In Proceedings of ACL 2005.*

Stuart Shieber, Yves Schabes, and Fernando Pereira. 1995. Principles and implementation of deductive parsing. *Journal of Logic Programming*, 24:3-15.

Andreas Stolcke. 2002. SRILM - an extensible language modeling toolkit. *In Proceedings of the International Conference on Spoken Language Processing*, volume 2, pages 901-904.

Ashish Venugopal, Andreas Zollmann, Stephan Vogel. 2007. An Efficient Two-Pass Approach to Synchronous-CFG Driven Statistical MT. *In Proceedings of NAACL 2007.*

Ying Zhang, Almut Silja Hildebrand, and Stephan Vogel. 2006. Distributed language modeling for n-best list reranking. *In Proceedings of EMNLP 2006.*

Prior Derivation Models For Formally Syntax-based Translation Using Linguistically Syntactic Parsing and Tree Kernels

Bowen Zhou
IBM T. J. Watson Research Center
Yorktown Heights, NY
zhou@us.ibm.com

Bing Xiang
IBM T. J. Watson Research Center
Yorktown Heights, NY
bxiang@us.ibm.com

Xiaodan Zhu
Dept. of Computer Science
University of Toronto
xzhu@cs.toronto.edu

Yuqing Gao
IBM T. J. Watson Research Center
Yorktown Heights, NY
yuqing@us.ibm.com

Abstract

This paper presents an improved formally syntax-based SMT model, which is enriched by linguistically syntactic knowledge obtained from statistical constituent parsers. We propose a linguistically-motivated prior derivation model to score hypothesis derivations on top of the baseline model during the translation decoding. Moreover, we devise a fast training algorithm to achieve such improved models based on tree kernel methods. Experiments on an English-to-Chinese task demonstrate that our proposed models outperformed the baseline formally syntax-based models, while both of them achieved significant improvements over a state-of-the-art phrase-based SMT system.

1 Introduction

In recent years, syntax-based translation models (Chiang, 2007; Galley et al., 2004; Liu et al., 2006) have shown promising progress in improving translation quality. There are two major elements accounting for such an improvement: namely the incorporation of phrasal translation structures adopted from widely applied phrase-based models (Och and Ney, 2004) to handle local fluency, and the engagement of synchronous context-free grammars (SCFG), which enhances the generative capacity of the underlying model that is limited by finite-state machinery.

Approaches to syntax-based translation models using SCFG can be further categorized into two classes, based on their dependency on annotated corpus. Following Chiang (Chiang, 2007), we note the following distinction between these two classes:

- *Linguistically* syntax-based: models that utilize structures defined over linguistic theory and annotations (e.g., Penn Treebank), and SCFG rules are derived from parallel corpus that is guided by explicitly parsing on at least one side of the parallel corpus. Examples among others are (Yamada and Knight, 2001) and (Galley et al., 2004).

- *Formally* syntax-based: models are based on hierarchical structures of natural language but synchronous grammars are automatically extracted from parallel corpus without any usage of linguistic knowledge or annotations. Examples include Wu's (Wu, 1997) ITG and Chiang's hierarchical models (Chiang, 2007).

While these two often resemble in appearance, from practical viewpoints, there are some distinctions in training and decoding procedures differentiating formally syntax-based models from linguistically syntax-based models. First, the former has no dependency on available linguistic theory and annotations for targeting language pairs, and thus the training and rule extraction are more efficient. Secondly, the decoding complexity of the former is lower [1], especially when integrating a n-gram based

[1] The complexity is dominated by synchronous parsing and boundary words keeping. Thus binary SCFG employed in formally syntax-based systems help to maintain efficient CKY decoding. Recent work by (Zhang et al., 2006) shows a practically efficient approach that binarizes linguistically SCFG rules when possible.

Proceedings of the Second ACL Workshop on Syntax and Structure in Statistical Translation (SSST-2), pages 19–27,
ACL-08: HLT, Columbus, Ohio, USA, June 2008.

language model, which is a key element to ensure translation output quality.

On the other hand, available linguistic theory and annotations could provide invaluable benefits in grammar induction and scoring, as shown by recent progress on such models (Galley et al., 2006). In contrast, formally syntax-based grammars often lack explicit linguistic constraints.

In this paper, we propose a scheme to enrich formally syntax-based models with linguistically syntactic knowledge. In other words, we maintain our grammar to be based on formal syntax on surface, but incorporate linguistic knowledge into our models to leverage syntax theory and annotations.

Our goal is two-fold. First, how to score SCFG rules whose general abstraction forms are unseen in the training data is an important question to answer. In hierarchical models, Chiang (Chiang, 2007) utilizes heuristics where certain assumptions are made on rule distributions to obtain relative frequency counts. We intend to explore if additional linguistically parsing information would be beneficial to improve the scoring of formally syntactic SCFG grammars. Secondly, we note that SCFG-based models often come with an excessive memory consumption as its rule size is an order of magnitude larger compared to phrase-based models, which challenges its practical deployment for online real-time translation tasks. Furthermore, formal syntax rules are often redundant as they are automatically extracted without linguistic supervision. Therefore, we are motivated to study approaches to further score and rank formal syntax rules based on syntax-inspired methods, and eventually to prune unnecessary rules without loss of performance in general.

In our study, we propose a linguistically-motivated method to train prior derivation models for formally syntax-based translation. In this framework, prior derivation models can be viewed as a smoothing of rule translation models, addressing the weakness of the baseline model estimation that relies on relative counts obtained from heuristics. First, we apply automatic parsers to obtain syntax annotations on the English side of the parallel corpus. Next, we extract tree fragments associated with phrase pairs, and measure similarity between such tree fragments using kernel methods (Collins and Duffy, 2002; Moschitti, 2006). Finally, we score and rank rules based on their minimal cluster similarity of their nonterminals, which is used to compute the prior distribution of hypothesis derivations during decoding for improved translation.

The remainder of the paper is organized as follows. We start with a brief review of some related work in Sec. 2. In Sec. 3, we describe our formally syntax-based models and decoder implementation, that is established as our baseline system. Sec. 4 presents the approach to score formal SCFG rules using kernel methods. Experimental results are provided in Sec. 5. Finally, Sec. 6 summarized our contributions with discussions and future work.

2 Related Work

Syntax-based translation models engaged with SCFG have been actively investigated in the literature (Wu, 1997; Yamada and Knight, 2001; Gildea, 2003; Galley et al., 2004; Satta and Peserico, 2005). Recent work by (Chiang, 2007; Galley et al., 2006) shows promising improvements compared to phrase-based models for large-scale tasks. However, few previous work directly applied linguistically syntactic information into a formally syntax-based models, which is explored in this paper.

Kernel methods leverage the fact that the only operation in a procedure is the evaluation of inner dot products between pairs of observations, where the inner product is thus replaced with a Mercer kernel that provides an efficient way to carry out computation when original feature dimension is large or even infinite. Collins and Duffy (Collins and Duffy, 2002) suggested to employ convolution kernels to measure similarity between two trees in terms of their substructures, and more recently, Moschitti (Moschitti, 2006) described in details a fast implementation of tree kernels. To our knowledge, this paper is one of the few efforts of applying kernel methods for improved translation.

3 Formally Syntax-based Models

An SCFG is a synchronous rewriting system generating source and target side string pairs simultaneously based on context-free grammar. Each synchronous production (i.e., rule) rewrites a nonterminal into a pair of strings, γ and α, with both terminals and nonterminals in both languages, subject to the constraint that there is a one-to-one correspondence between nonterminal occurrences on the source and target side. In particular, formally syntax-based models explore hierarchical structures of natural language and utilize only a unified nonterminal symbol X in the grammar,

$$X \rightarrow \langle \gamma, \alpha, \sim \rangle, \quad (1)$$

where $\sim$ is the one-to-one correspondence between X's in γ and α, which is indicated by underscripted co-indices on both sides. For example, some English-to-Chinese production rules can be represented as follows:

$$X \rightarrow \langle X_1 \text{enjoy reading} X_2, \quad (2)$$
$$X_1 \text{xihuan}(\textit{enjoy}) \text{ yuedu}(\textit{reading}) X_2 \rangle$$
$$X \rightarrow \langle X_1 \text{enjoy reading} X_2,$$
$$X_1 \text{xihuan}(\textit{enjoy}) X_2 \text{yuedu}(\textit{reading}) \rangle$$

The set of rules, denoted as $\mathcal{R}$, are automatically extracted from sentence-aligned parallel corpus (Chiang, 2007). First, bidirectional word-level alignment is carried out on the parallel corpus running GIZA++ (Och and Ney, 2000). Based on the resulting Viterbi alignments A_{e2f} and A_{f2e}, the union, $A_U = A_{e2f} \cup A_{f2e}$, is taken as the symmetrized word-level alignment. Next, bilingual phrase pairs consistent with word alignments are extracted from A_U (Och and Ney, 2004). Specifically, any pair of consecutive sequences of words below a maximum length M is considered to be a phrase pair if its component words are aligned only within the phrase pair and not to any words outside. The resulting bilingual phrase pair inventory is denoted as $\mathcal{BP}$. Each phrase pair PP $\in \mathcal{BP}$ is represented as a production rule $X \rightarrow \langle f_i^j, e_k^l \rangle$, which we refer to as *phrasal rules*. The SCFG rule set encloses all phrase pairs, i.e., $\mathcal{BP} \subset \mathcal{R}$. Next, we loop through each phrase pair PP and generalize the sub-phrase pair contained in PP, denoted as SP_e and SP_f subject to $\text{SP} = (\text{SP}_f, \text{SP}_e) \in \mathcal{BP}$, with co-indexed nonterminal symbols. We thereby obtain a new rule.

We limit the number of nonterminals in each rule no more than two, thus ensuring the rank of SCFG is two. To reduce rule size and spurious ambiguity, we apply constraints described in (Chiang, 2007). In addition, we require that the sub-phrases being abstracted by correspondent nonterminals have to be aligned together in the original phrase pair, which significantly reduces the number of rules. We will hereafter refer to rules with nonterminal symbols as *abstract rules* to distinguish them from phrasal rules. Finally, an implicit *glue* rule is embedded with decoder to allow for translations that can be achieved by sequentially linking sub-translations generated chunk-by-chunk:

$$X \rightarrow \langle X_1 X_2, X_1 X_2 \rangle. \quad (3)$$

That is, X is also our sentence start symbol.

During such a rule extraction procedure, we note that there is a many-to-many mapping between phrase pairs (contiguous word sequences without nonterminals) and derived rules (a mixed combination of word and nonterminal sequences). In other words, one original phrase pair can induce a number of different rules, and the same rule can also be derived from a number of different phrase pairs.

3.1 Models

All rules in $\mathcal{R}$ are paired with statistical parameters (i.e., weighted SCFG), which combines with other features to form our models using a log-linear framework. Translation using SCFG for an input sentence f is casted as to find the optimal derivation on source and target side (as the grammar is synchronous, the derivations on source and target sides are identical). By "optimal", it indicates that the derivation D maximizes following log-linear models over all possible derivations:

$$P(D) \propto P_{LM}(e)^{\lambda_{LM}} \times$$
$$\prod_i \prod_{X \rightarrow <\gamma, \alpha> \in D} \phi_i(X \rightarrow <\gamma, \alpha>)^{\lambda_i}, \quad (4)$$

where the set of $\phi_i(X \rightarrow <\gamma, \alpha>)$ are features defined over given production rule, and $P_{LM}(e)$ is the language model score on hypothesized output, the λ_i is the feature weight.

Our baseline model follows Chiang's hierarchical model (Chiang, 2007) in conjunction with additional features:

- conditional probabilities in both directions: $P(\gamma|\alpha)$ and $P(\alpha|\gamma)$;
- lexical weights (Koehn et al., 2003) in both directions: $P_w(\gamma|\alpha)$ and $P_w(\alpha|\gamma)$;

- word counts $|e|$;
- rule counts $|D|$;
- target n-gram language model $P_{LM}(e)$;
- glue rule penalty to learn preference of nonterminal rewriting over serial combination through Eq. 3;

Moreover, we propose an additional feature, namely the *abstraction penalty*, to account for the accumulated number of nonterminals applied in D:

- abstraction penalty $exp(-N_a)$, where $N_a = \sum_{X \rightarrow <\gamma,\alpha> \in D} n(\gamma)$

where $n(\gamma)$ is the number of nonterminals in γ. This feature aims to learn the preference among phrasal rules, and abstract rules with one or two nonterminals. This makes our syntax-based model includes a total of nine features.

The training procedure described in (Chiang, 2007) employs heuristics to hypothesize a distribution of possible rules. A count one is assigned to every phrase pair occurrence, which is equally distributed among rules that are derived from this phrase pair. Hypothesizing this distribution as our observations on rule occurrence, relative-frequency estimation is used to obtain $P(\gamma|\alpha)$ and $P(\alpha|\gamma)$.

We note that, however, these parameters are often poorly estimated due to the usage of inaccurate heuristics, which is the major problem that we alleviate in Sec. 4.

3.2 Decoder

The objective of our syntax-based decoder is to search for the optimal derivation tree D from a forest of trees that can represent the input sentence. The target side is mapped accordingly at each nonterminal node in the tree, and a traverse of these nodes obtains the target translation. Fig. 1 shows an example for chart parsing that produces the translation from the best parse.

Our decoder implements a modified CKY parser in C++ with integrated n-gram language model scoring. During search, chart cells are filled in a bottom-up fashion until a tree rooted from nonterminal is generated that covers the entire input sentence. The dynamic programming item we bookkeep is denoted and asterisk denotes arbitrary symbol sequences on the other side consistent with our grammars [2]. The production of $L(\cdot)$ over all rules observed in a derivation D measures the prior distribution of D. In the baseline model, as a special case, we can see that $L(\cdot)$ is a constant function.

The motivation is straightforward since some derivations should be preferred over others. One may make an analogy between our prior derivation distributions to non-uniform source side segmentation models in phrase-based systems. However, it should be noted that prior derivation models influence not only on phrase choices as what segmentation models do, but also on ordering options due to the nonterminal usage in syntax-based models.

In principle, some quantitative schemes are needed to evaluate the monolingual derivation prior probability. Our scheme links the source side derivation prior probability with the expected ambiguity on target side generation when mapping the source side to target side given the derivation. That is, a given source side derivation is favored if it introduces less ambiguity on target generation compared to others.

Let us revisit the rules in Eq. 2. We notice that the same source side maps into different target orders depending on the *syntactic role* (e.g., NP or PP) of X_2 in the rule. Furthermore, the following are example rules trained from real data (see Sec. 5):

$$X \rightarrow \langle X_1 \text{pass} X_2, X_1 \text{gei } (\textit{give}) X_2 \rangle \quad (6)$$

$$X \rightarrow \langle X_1 \text{pass} X_2, X_1 \text{jingguo } (\textit{traverse}) X_2 \rangle \quad (7)$$

$$X \rightarrow \langle X_1 \text{pass} X_2, X_1 \text{piao } (\textit{ticket}) X_2 \rangle \quad (8)$$

Above three rules cover pretty well for different usages of *pass* in English and its correspondence in Chinese. Typically, applying the rule to inputs such as "my pass *expired*" obtains reasonable translations with baseline models. However, it will fail on inputs like "my pass *to the zoo*" as none of th rules provides a correct translation of X_1X_2piao (*ticket*) when X_2 is a prepositional phrase.

Such linguistic phenomena, among others, indicates that the higher variation of syntax structures the nonterminal embodies, the more translation options on target side needed to account for various syntactic roles on source side. This suggests that our prior derivation models should prefer nonterminals that cover more syntactically homogeneous constituents. Such a model is thus proposed in Sec. 4.1.

The prior derivation model can also be viewed as a smoothing on rule translation probabilities estimated using heuristics, as we mentioned in Sec. 3.1. When there are more translation options, we deem that there are more ambiguity for this rule. In cases where some dominating translation option is overestimated from hypothesized distributions, all translation options of this rule are discounted as they are less favored by prior derivation models.

4.1 Model Syntactic Variations

Each abstract rule is generalized from a set of original relevant phrase pairs by grouping an appropriate set of sub-phrases into a nonterminal symbol, with each sub-phrase linked to a tree list. Therefore, the joined tree lists form a forest for this nonterminal symbol in the rule. For every abstract rule, we define the rule forest to be the set of tree fragments of all sub-phrases abstracted within this rule.

We parse the English side of parallel corpus to obtain a syntactic tree for each English sentence. For each phrase extracted from this sentence, we define the *tree fragment* for this phrase as the minimal set of internal tree whose leaves span exactly over this phrase. As a common practice, we preserve all phrase pairs in $\mathcal{BP}$ including those who are not consistent with parser sub-trees. Therefore, there will be many phrases that cross over syntactic sub-trees, which subsequently produced tree fragments lacking a root. We label those as "incomplete" tree fragments, and introduce a parent node of "INC" on top of them to form a single-rooted subtree. For example, Fig. 2 shows the tree fragments for phrases of "reading books" and "enjoy reading", where the latter is an "incomplete" tree fragment. Moreover, for sentences failed on parsing, we label all phrases extracted from those sentences with a root of "EMPTY".

Subset trees of tree fragments are defined as any sub-graph that contains more than one nodes, with the restriction that entire rule productions must be

[2]In general, we can plug in either $L(X \rightarrow < \gamma, * >)$ or $L(X \rightarrow < *, \alpha >)$ here. For illustration purposes, we assume that the model is on the source side.

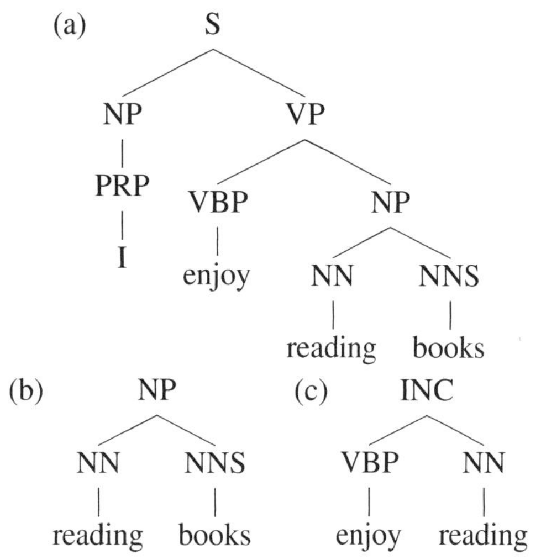

Figure 2: Syntax parsing tree (a) and tree fragments for phrases "reading books" (b) and "enjoy reading" (c).

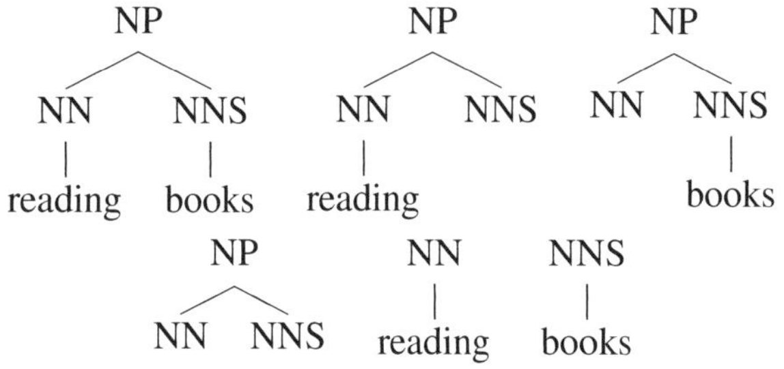

Figure 3: Subset trees of the NP covering "reading books".

included (Collins and Duffy, 2002). Fig. 3 enumerates a list of subset trees for fragment (b) in Fig. 2.

To measure syntactic homogeneity, we define the fragment similarity $K(T_1, T_2)$ as the number of common subset trees between two tree fragments T_1 and T_2. Conceptually, if we enumerate all possible subset trees $1, \ldots, M$, we can represent each tree fragment T as a vector $h(T) = (c_1, \ldots, c_M)$ with each element as the count of occurrences of each subset tree in T. Thus, the similarity can be expressed by the inner products of these two vectors. Note that M will be a huge number for our problem, and thus we need kernel methods presented below to make computation tractable.

4.2 Kernel Methods

Collins and Duffy (Collins and Duffy, 2002) introduced a method employing convolution kernels to measure similarity between two trees in terms of their sub-structures. If we define an indicator function $I_i(n)$ to be 1 if subset tree i is rooted at node n and 0 otherwise, we have:

$$K(T_1, T_2) = \sum_{n_1 \in N_1} \sum_{n_2 \in N_2} C(n_1, n_2) \quad (9)$$

where $C(n_1, n_2) = \sum_i I_i(n_1) I_i(n_2)$ and N_1, N_2 are the set of nodes in the tree fragment T_1 and T_2 respectively. It is noted that $C(n_1, n_2)$ can be computed recursively (Collins and Duffy, 2002):

1. $C(n_1, n_2) = 0$ if the productions at n_1 and n_2 are different;
2. $C(n_1, n_2) = 1$ if the productions at n_1 and n_2 are the same and both are pre-terminals;
3. Otherwise,

$$C(n_1, n_2) = \lambda \prod_{j=1}^{nc(n_1)} (1 + C(ch_{n_1}^j, ch_j^{n_2})) \quad (10)$$

where $ch_{n_1}^j$ is the jth child of node n_1, $nc(n_1)$ is the number of children at n_1 and $0 < \lambda \leq 1$ is a decay factor to discount the effects of deeper tree structures.

In principle, the computational complexity of Eq. 10 is $\mathcal{O}(|N_1| \times |N_2|)$. However, as noted by (Collins and Duffy, 2002), the worst case is quite uncommon to natural language syntactic trees. More recently, Moschitti (Moschitti, 2006) introduced in details a fast implementation of tree kernels, where a node pair set is first constructed for those associated with same production rules. Our work follows Moschitti's implementation, which runs in linear time on average. We compute the normalized similarity as $K'(T_1, T_2) = \frac{K(T_1, T_2)}{\sqrt{K(T_1, T_1)} \times \sqrt{K(T_2, T_2)}}$ to ensure similarity is normalized between 0 and 1.

4.3 Prior Derivation Cost

First we define the purity of a nonterminal forest (with respect to a given rule) $Pur(X)$ as the average similarity of all tree fragments in the cluster:

$$Pur(X) = \frac{2}{N(N-1)} \sum_j \sum_{i<j} K'(T_i, T_j), \quad (11)$$

where N is number of tree fragments in the forest of X. We now can define the derivation cost $L(X \rightarrow <$

$\gamma, * >)$ for a rule production as:

$$L(X \rightarrow< \gamma, * >) = \\ -\log((\min_{X_1, X_2 \in \gamma} (Pur(X_1), Pur(X_2)))^k), \quad (12)$$

where $k \geq 1$ is the degree of smoothness. Note that the prior derivation cost is set as $L(\cdot) = 0$ by definition for phrasal rules.

Eq. 11 is quadratic complexity with N, however, we note that rules with a large N will typically score poorly on prior derivation models, and thus we can avoid the computation for those by assigning them a large cost. With the fast kernel computation, the training procedure involved with the prior derivation models for the task presented in Sec. 5 is about 5 times slower on a single machine, compared with the training of the baseline system. However, we note that our training procedure can be computed in parallel, and therefore the training speed is not a bottleneck when multiple CPUs are available.

5 Experiments

We perform our experiments on an English-to-Chinese translation task in travel domain. Our training set contains 482017 parallel sentences (with 4.4M words on the English side), which are collected from transcription and human translation of conversations. The vocabulary size is 37K for English and 44K for Chinese after segmentation.

Our evaluation data is a held out data set of 2755 sentences pairs. We extracted every one out of two sentence pairs into the dev-set, and left the remainder as the test-set. We thereby obtained a dev-set of 1378 sentence pairs, and a test-set with 1377 sentence pairs. In both cases, there are about 15K running words on English side. All Chinese sentences in training, dev and test sets are all automatically segmented into words. Minimum-error-rate training (Och, 2003) are conducted on dev-set to optimize feature weights maximizing the BLEU score up to 4-grams, and the obtained feature weights are blindly applied on the test-set. To compare performances excluding tokenization effects, all BLEU scores are optimized (on dev-set) and reported (on test-set) at Chinese character-level.

From training data, we extracted an initial phrase pair set with 3.7M entries for phrases up to 8 words on Chinese side. We trained a 4-gram language model for Chinese at word level, which is shared by all translation systems reported in this paper, using the Chinese side of the parallel corpus that contains around 2M segmented words.

We compare the proposed models with two baselines: a state-of-the-art phrase-based system and a formal syntax-based system as described in Sec. 3. The phrase-based system employs the 3.7M phrase pairs to build the translation model, and it contains a total set of 8 features, most of which are identical to our baseline formal syntax-based model. The difference only lies on that the glue and abstraction penalty are not applicable for phrase-based system. Instead, a lexicalized reordering model is trained from the word-aligned parallel corpus for the phrase-based system. More details about our multiple-graph based phrasal SMT can be found in (Zhou et al., 2006; Zhou et al., 2008). For the baseline syntax-based system, we generated a total of 15M rules and used 9 features.

We chose the Stanford parser (Klein and Manning, 2002) as the English parser in our experiments due to its high accuracy and relatively faster speed. It was trained on the Wall Street Journal section of the Penn Treebank. During the parsing, the input English sentences were tokenized first, in a style consistent with the data in the Penn Treebank.

We sent 482017 English sentences to the parser. There were 1221 long sentences failed, less than 0.3% of the whole set. After the word alignment and phrase extraction on the parallel corpus, we obtained 2.2M unique English phrases. Among them there are about 34K phrases having an empty tree in their corresponding tree lists, due to the failure in parsing. The number of unique tree fragments for English phrases is 2.5M. Out of them there are 750K marked as incomplete. As mentioned previously, each rule covers a set of phrases, with each phrase linked to a tree list. The total number of rules with unique English side is around 8M.

The distribution of the number of rules over the number of corresponding trees is shown in Table 1. We observe that the majority of rules in our model has less than 150 tree fragments. Therefore, considering the quadratic complexity in Eq. 11, we punish the rules with more than 150 unique tree fragments with some floor cluster purity to speed up

Table 1: Distribution of rules over trees

Number of trees	Number of rules
$(0, 10]$	3636766
$(10, 20]$	1556806
$(20, 30]$	989848
$(30, 40]$	916606
$(40, 50]$	488469
$(50, 60]$	270484
$(60, 70]$	198438
$(70, 80]$	86921
$(80, 90]$	58280
$(90, 100]$	29147
$(100, 150]$	437231
> 150	81060

the training. Not surprisingly, the rules with a large number of tree fragments are typically those with few stop words as terminals. For instance, the rule $X \rightarrow< X_1 \text{a} X_2, * >$ comes with more than 100K trees for the X_1.

Table 2: English-to-Chinese BLEU score result on test-set (character-based)

Models	BLEU(4-gram)
Phrase-based	42.11
Formally Syntax-based	43.75
Formally Syntax-based with prior derivation	44.51

Translation results are presented in Table 2 with character-based BLEU scores using 2 references. Our baseline formally syntax-based models achieved the BLEU score of 43.75, an absolute improvement of 1.6 point improvement over phrase-based models. The improvement is statistically significant with $p < 0.01$ using the sign-test described by (Collins et al., 2005). Applying the prior derivation model into the syntax-based system, BLEU score is further improved to 44.51, obtained an another absolute improvement of 0.8 point, which is also significantly better than our baseline syntax-based models ($p < 0.05$).

6 Discussion and Summary

We introduced a prior derivation model to enhance formally syntax-based SCFG for translation. Our approach links a prior rule distribution with the syntactic variations of abstracted sub-phrases, which is modeled by distance measuring of linguistically syntax parsing tree fragments using kernel methods. The proposed model has improved translation performance over both phrase-based and formally syntax-based models. Moreover, such a prior distribution can also be used to rank and prune SCFG rules to reduce memory usage for online translation systems based on syntax-based models.

Although the experiments in this paper are conducted for prior derivation models on source side in an English-to-Chinese task, we are interested in applying this to foreign-to-English models as well. As what we pointed out in Sec. 4, target side prior derivation model fits with our framework as well.

7 Acknowledgement

The authors would like to thank Stanley F. Chen and the anonymous reviewers for their helpful comments on this paper.

References

David Chiang. 2007. Hierarchical phrase-based translation. *Comput. Linguist.*, 33(2):201–228.

Michael Collins and Nigel Duffy. 2002. Convolution kernels for natural language. In *Advances in Neural Information Processing Systems 14*.

Michael Collins, Philipp Koehn, and Ivona Kučerová. 2005. Clause restructuring for statistical machine translation. In *Proc. of ACL*, pages 531–540.

Michel Galley, Mark Hopkins, Kevin Knight, and Daniel Marcu. 2004. What's in a translation rule? In *Proc. of HLT/NAACL-04*, Boston, USA, May.

Michel Galley, Jonathan Graehl, Kevin Knight, Daniel Marcu, Steve DeNeefe, Wei Wang, and Ignacio Thayer. 2006. Scalable inference and training of context-rich syntactic translation models. In *Proc. of ACL*, pages 961–968.

Daniel Gildea. 2003. Loosely tree-based alignment for machine translation. In *Proc. of ACL*, pages 80–87.

Dan Klein and Christopher D. Manning. 2002. Fast exact inference with a factored model for natural language parsing. In *NIPS*, pages 3–10.

Philipp Koehn, Franz Och, and Daniel Marcu. 2003. Statistical phrase-based translation. In *Proc. NAACL/HLT*.

Yang Liu, Qun Liu, and Shouxun Lin. 2006. Tree-to-string alignment template for statistical machine translation. In *Proc. of ACL*, pages 609–616.

Alessandro Moschitti. 2006. Making tree kernels practical for natural language learning. In *Proc. of EACL.*

F. J. Och and H. Ney. 2000. Improved statistical alignment models. In *Proc. of ACL*, pages 440–447, Hong Kong, China, October.

Franz Josef Och and Hermann Ney. 2004. The alignment template approach to statistical machine translation. *Comput. Linguist.*, 30(4):417–449.

Franz Josef Och. 2003. Minimum error rate training in statistical machine translation. In *Proc. of ACL*, pages 160–167.

Giorgio Satta and Enoch Peserico. 2005. Some computational complexity results for synchronous context-free grammars. In *Proc. of HLT/EMNLP*, pages 803–810.

Dekai Wu. 1997. Stochastic inversion transduction grammars and bilingual parsing of parallel corpora. *Comput. Linguist.*, 23(3):377–403.

Kenji Yamada and Kevin Knight. 2001. A syntax-based statistical translation model. In *Proc. of ACL*, pages 523–530.

Hao Zhang, Liang Huang, Daniel Gildea, and Kevin Knight. 2006. Synchronous binarization for machine translation. In *Proc. of HLT/NAACL*, pages 256–263.

Bowen Zhou, Stan F. Chen, and Yuqing Gao. 2006. Folsom: A fast and memory-efficient phrase-based approach to statistical machine translation. In *IEEE/ACL Workshop on Spoken Language Technology*.

Bowen Zhou, Rong Zhang, and Yuqing Gao. 2008. Lexicalized reordering in multiple-graph based statistical machine translation. In *Proc. ICASSP*.

Generalizing local translation models

Michael Subotin
Laboratory for Computational Linguistics and Information Processing
Department of Linguistics
University of Maryland
College Park, MD 20742
msubotin@umiacs.umd.edu

Abstract

We investigate translation modeling based on exponential estimates which generalize essential components of standard translation models. In application to a hierarchical phrase-based system the simplest generalization allows its models of lexical selection and reordering to be conditioned on arbitrary attributes of the source sentence and its annotation. Viewing these estimates as approximations of sentence-level probabilities motivates further elaborations that seek to exploit general syntactic and morphological patterns. Dimensionality control with ℓ_1 regularizers makes it possible to negotiate the tradeoff between translation quality and decoding speed. Putting together and extending several recent advances in phrase-based translation we arrive at a flexible modeling framework that allows efficient leveraging of monolingual resources and tools. Experiments with features derived from the output of Chinese and Arabic parsers and an Arabic lemmatizer show significant improvements over a strong baseline.

1 Introduction

Effective handling of large and diverse inventories of feature functions is one of the most pressing open problems in machine translation. While minimum error training (Och, 2003) has by now become a standard tool for interpolating a small number of aggregate scores, it is not well suited for learning in high-dimensional feature spaces. At the same time, although recent years have seen considerable progress in development of general methods for large-scale prediction of complex outputs (Bakır et al., 2007), their application to language translation has presented considerable challenges. Several studies have shown that large-margin methods can be adapted to the special complexities of the task (Liang et al., 2006; Tillmann and Zhang, 2006; Cowan et al., 2006) . However, the capacity of these algorithms to improve over state-of-the-art baselines is currently limited by their lack of robust dimensionality reduction. Performance gains are closely tied to the number and variety of candidate features that enter into the model, and increasing the size of the feature space not only slows down training in terms of the number of iterations required for convergence, but can also considerably reduce decoding speed, leading to run-time costs that may be unacceptable in industrial settings. Vector space regression has shown impressive performance in other tasks involving string-to-string mappings (Cortes et al., 2007), but its application to language translation presents a different set of open problems (Wang et al., 2007). Other promising formalisms, which have not yet produced end-to-end systems competitive with standard baselines, include the approach due to Turian et al (2006), the hidden-state synchronous grammar-based exponential model studied by Blunsom et al (2008), and a similar model incorporating target-side n-gram features proposed in Subotin (2008).

Taken together the results of these studies point to a striking overarching conclusion: the humble relative frequency estimate of phrase-based models makes for a surprisingly strong baseline. The present paper investigates a family of models that

Proceedings of the Second ACL Workshop on Syntax and Structure in Statistical Translation (SSST-2), pages 28–36,
ACL-08: HLT, Columbus, Ohio, USA, June 2008.

capitalize on this practical insight to allow efficient optimization of weights for a virtually unlimited number of features. We take as a point of departure the observation that the essential translation model scores comprising standard decoding decision rules can be recovered as special cases of a more general family of models. As we discuss below, they are equal to maximum likelihood solutions for locally normalized "piecewise" approximations to sentence-level probabilities, where word alignment is used to determine the subset of features observed in each training example. The cases for which such solutions have a closed form correspond to particular restrictions placed on the feature space. Thus, relative frequency phrase models can be obtained by limiting the feature space to indicator functions for the phrase pairs consistent with an alignment. By removing unnecessary restrictions we restore the full flexibility of local exponential models, including their ability to use features depending on arbitrary aspects of the source sentence and its annotation. The availability of robust algorithms for dimensionality reduction with ℓ_1 regularizers (Ng, 2004) means that we can start with a virtually unlimited number of candidate features and negotiate the tradeoff between translation quality and decoding speed in a way appropriate for a given setting. A further attractive property of locally normalized models is the modest computational cost of their training and ease of its parallelization. This is particularly so for the models we concentrate on in this paper, defined so that parameter estimation decomposes into a large number of small optimization subproblems which can be solved independently.

Several variants of these models beyond relative frequencies have appeared in the literature before. Maximum entropy estimation for translation of individual words dates back to Berger et al (1996), and the idea of using multi-class classifiers to sharpen predictions normally made through relative frequency estimates has been recently reintroduced under the rubric of word sense disambiguation and generalized to substrings (Chan et al 2007; Carpuat and Wu 2007a; Carpuat and Wu 2007b). Maximum entropy models for non-lexicalized reordering rules for a phrase-based system with CKY decoding has been described by Xiong et al (2006). Some of our experiments, where exponential models conditioned on the source sentence and its parse annotation are associated with all rewrite rules in a hierarchical phrase-based system (Chiang, 2007) and all word-level probabilities in standard lexical models, may be seen as a synthesis of these ideas.

The broader perspective of viewing the product of such local probabilities as a particular approximation of sentence-level likelihood points the way beyond multi-class classification, and this type of generalization is the main original contribution of the present work. Training a classifier to predict the target phrase for every source phrase is equivalent to conjoining all contextual features of the model with an indicator function for the surface form of some rule in the grammar. We can also use features based on less specific representation of a rule. Of particular importance for machine translations are representations which generalize reordering information beyond identity of individual words – a type of generalization that presents a challenge in hierarchical phrase-based translation. With generalized local models this can be accomplished by adding features tracking only ordering patterns of rules. We experiment with a case of such models which allows us to preserve decomposition of parameter estimation into independent subproblems.

Besides varying the structure of the feature space, we can also extend the range of normalization for the exponential models beyond target phrases cooccurring with a given source phrase in the phrase table. This choice is especially natural for richly inflected languages, since it enables us to model multiple levels of morphological representation at once and estimate probabilities for rules whose surface forms have not been observed in training. We apply a simple variant of this approach to Arabic-English lexical models.

Experimental results across eight test sets in two language pairs support the intuition that features conjoined with indicator functions for surface forms of rules yield higher gains for test sets with better coverage in training data, while features based on less specific representations become more useful for test sets with lower baselines.

The types of features explored in this paper represent only a small portion of available options, and much practical experimentation remains to be done, particularly in order to find the most effective extensions of the feature space beyond multiclass classification. However, the results reported here show considerable promise and we believe that the flexibility of these models combined with their computational efficiency makes them potentially valuable as an extension for a variety of systems using translation models with local conditional probabilities and as a feature selection method for globally trained models.

2 Hierarchical phrase-based translation

We take as our starting point David Chiang's Hiero system, which generalizes phrase-based translation to substrings with gaps (Chiang, 2007). Consider for instance the following set of context-free rules with a single non-terminal symbol:

$$\langle A, A \rangle \rightarrow \langle A_1 A_2 , A_1 A_2 \rangle$$
$$\langle A, A \rangle \rightarrow \langle d' A_1 \textit{idées} A_2 , A_1 A_2 \textit{ideas} \rangle$$
$$\langle A, A \rangle \rightarrow \langle \textit{incolores} , \textit{colorless} \rangle$$
$$\langle A, A \rangle \rightarrow \langle \textit{vertes} , \textit{green} \rangle$$
$$\langle A, A \rangle \rightarrow \langle \textit{dorment}\, A , \textit{sleep}\, A \rangle$$
$$\langle A, A \rangle \rightarrow \langle \textit{furieusement} , \textit{furiously} \rangle$$

It is one of many rule sets that would suffice to generate the English translation 1b for the French sentence 1a.

1a. *d' incolores idées vertes dorment furieusement*
1b. *colorless green ideas sleep furiously*

As shown by Chiang (2007), a weighted grammar of this form can be collected and scored by simple extensions of standard methods for phrase-based translation and efficiently combined with a language model in a CKY decoder to achieve large improvements over a state-of-the-art phrase-based system. The translation is chosen to be the target-side yield of the highest-scoring synchronous parse consistent with the source sentence. Although a variety of scores interpolated into the decision rule for phrase-based systems have been investigated over the years, only a handful have been discovered to be consistently useful, as is in our experience also the case for the hierarchical variant. Setting aside specialized components such as number translators, we concentrate on the essential sub-models[1] comprising the translation model: the phrase models and lexical models.

3 Local exponential translation models

3.1 Relative frequency solutions

Standard phrase models associate conditional probabilities with subparts of translation hypotheses, usually computed as relative frequencies of counts of extracted phrases.[2] Let r^y be the target side of a rule and r^x its source side. The weight of the rule in the "reverse" phrase model would then be computed as

$$p(r^y|r^x) = \frac{count(\langle r^x, r^y \rangle)}{\sum_{r^{y'}} count(\langle r^x, r^{y'} \rangle)} \quad (1)$$

When used to score a translation hypothesis corresponding to some synchronous parse tree T, the phrase model may be conceived as an approximation of the probability of a target sentence Y given a source sentence X

$$p(Y|X) \approx \prod_{r \in T} p(r^y|r^x) \quad (2)$$

Although there is nothing in current learning theory that would prompt one to expect that expressions of this form should be effective, their surprisingly strong performance in machine translation in an empirical observation borne out by many studies. In order to build on this practical insight it is useful to gain a clearer understanding of their formal properties.

We start by writing out an expression for the likelihood of training data which would give rise to maximum likelihood solutions like those in eq. 1. Consider a feature vector whose components are indicator functions for rules in the grammar, and let us define an exponential model for a sentence pair (X_m, Y_m) of the form

$$p \quad (Y_m|X_m) \approx \prod_{r \in (X_m, Y_m)} p(r^y|r^x) \quad (3)$$

$$= \prod_{r \in (X_m, Y_m)} \frac{exp\{\mathbf{w} \cdot \mathbf{f}_r(X_m, Y_m)\}}{\sum_{\tilde{r}: r^x = \tilde{r}^x} exp\{\mathbf{w} \cdot \mathbf{f}_{\tilde{r}}(X_m, Y_m)\}} \quad (4)$$

[1]To avoid confusion with features of the exponential models described below we shall use the term "model" for the terms interpolated using MERT.

[2]Chiang (2007) uses a heuristic estimate of fractional counts in these computations. For completeness we report both variants in the experiments.

where $\mathbf{f}_r(X_m, Y_m)$ is a restriction of the feature vector such that all of its entries except for the one corresponding to the rule r are zero and the summation is over all rules in the grammar with the same source side. As can be verified by writing out the likelihood for the training set and setting its gradient to zero, maximum likelihood estimation based on eq. 4 yields estimates equal to relative frequency solutions. In fact, because its normalization factors have non-zero parameters in common only for rules which share the same source phrase, parameter estimation decomposes into independent optimization subproblems, one for each source phrase in the grammar. However, recovering relative frequencies of the needed form requires further attention to the relationship between the definition of feature functions and phrase extraction. Computation of phrase models in machine translation crucially relies on a form of feature selection not widely known in other contexts. A rule is considered to be observed in a sentence pair only if it is consistent with predictions of a word alignment model according to heuristics for alignment combination and phrase extraction. The standard recipes in translation modeling can thus be seen to include a feature selection procedure that applies *individually* to each training example.

3.2 Classifier solutions

We can now generalize these relative frequency estimates by relaxing the restrictions they implicitly place on the form of permissible feature functions. The simplest elaboration involves allowing indicator functions for rules to be conjoined with indicator functions for arbitrary attributes of the source sentence or its annotation. This preserves a decomposition of parameter estimation of optimization subproblems associated with individual source phrase, but effectively replaces probabilities $p(r^y|r^x)$ in eqs. 2 and 3 with probabilities conditioned on the source phrase together with some of its source-side context. We may, for example, conjoin an indicator function for the rule $\langle A, A \rangle \rightarrow \langle\, d'\, A_1\, idées\, A_2\,,\, A_1\, A_2\, ideas \,\rangle$ with a function telling us whether a part-of-speech tagger has identified the word at the left edge of the source-side gap A_2 as an adjective, which would provide additional evidence for the target side of this rule. Combining a grammar-based formalism with contextual features raises a subtle question of whether rules which have gaps at the edges and can match at multiple positions of a training example should be counted as having occurred together with their respective contextual features once for each possible match. To avoid favoring monotone rules, which tend to match at many positions, over reordering rules, which tend to match at a single span, we randomly sample only one of such multiple matches for training.

Unlike conventional phrase models, contextually-conditioned probabilities cannot be stored in a pre-computed phrase table. Instead, we store information about features and their weights and compute the normalization factors at run-time at the point when they are first needed by the decoder.

At the expense of more complicated decoding procedures we could also apply the same line of reasoning to generalize the "noisy channel" phrase model $p(r^x|r^y)$ to be conditioned on local target-side context in a translation hypothesis, possibly combining target-side annotation of the training set with surface form of rules. We do not pursue this elaboration in part because we are skeptical about its potential for success. The current state of machine translation rarely permits constructing well-formed translations, so that most of the contextual features on the target side would be rarely if at all observed in the training data, resulting in sparse and noisy estimates. Furthermore, we have yet to find a case where relative frequency estimates $p(r^x|r^y)$ make a useful contribution to the system when contextually-conditioned "reverse" probabilities are used, suggesting that viewing translation modeling as approximating sentence-level probabilities $p(Y|X)$ may be a more fruitful avenue in the long term.

For translation with phrases without gaps classifier solutions of eq. 4 are equivalent to a maximum entropy variant of the *phrase sense disambiguation* approach studied by Carpuat & Wu (2007b). These solutions are also closely related to the approximation known as *piecewise training* in graphical model literature (Sutton and McCallum, 2005; Sutton and Minka, 2006) and independently stated in a more general form by Pérez-Cruz et al (2007). Aside from formal differences between feature templates defined by graphical models and grammars, which are beyond the scope of our discussion, there are several further contrasts between these studies and standard practice in machine translation in how the learned parameters are used to make predictions. Unlike inference in piecewise-trained graphical models, where all parameters for a given output are added together without normalization, features that enter into the score for a translation hypothesis are restricted to be consistent with a single synchronous parse and the local probabilities are normalized in decoding as in training.

3.3 Lexical models

The use of conditional probabilities in standard lexical models also gives us a straightforward way to generalize them in the same way as phrase models. Consider the lexical model $p_w(r^y|r^x)$, defined following Koehn et al (2003), with a denoting the most frequent word alignment observed for the rule in the training set.

$$p_w(r^y|r^x) = \prod_{i=1}^{n} \frac{1}{|j|(i,j) \in a|} \sum_{(i,j)\in a} p(w_i^y|w_j^x) \tag{5}$$

We replace $p(w_i^y|w_j^x)$ with context-conditioned probabilities, computed similarly to eq. 4, but at the level of individual words. Our experience suggests that, unlike the analogous phrase model, the standard lexical model $p_w(r^x|r^y)$ is not made redundant by this elaboration, and we use its baseline variant in all our experiments. While this approach seeks to make the most of practical insights underlying state-of-the-art baselines, it is of course not the only way to combine rule-based and word-based features. See for example Sutton & Minka (2006) for a discussion of alternatives that are closer in spirit to the idea of approximating global probabilities.

3.4 Further generalizations

An immediate practical benefit of interpreting relative frequency and classifier estimates of translation models as special cases is the possibility of generalizing them further by introducing additional features based on less specific representations of rules and words.

Among the least specific and most potentially useful representations of hierarchical phrases are those limited to the patterns formed by gaps and words, allowing the model to generalize reordering information beyond individual tokens. We study two types of ordering patterns. For rules with two gaps we form features by conjoining contextual indicator functions with functions indicating whether the gap pattern is monotone or inverting. We also use another type of ordering features, representing the pattern formed by gaps and contiguous subsequences of words. For example, the rule with the right-hand side $\langle\ d'\ A_1\ id\acute{e}es\ A_2\ ,\ A_1\ A_2\ ideas\ \rangle$ might be associated with the pattern $\langle\ a\ A_1\ a\ A_2\ ,\ A_1\ A_2\ a\ \rangle$. Because some source-side patterns of this type apply to many different rules it is no longer possible to decompose parameter estimation into small independent optimization subproblems. For practical convenience we enforce decomposition in the experiments reported below in the following way. We define indicator functions for sequences of closed-class words and the most frequent part-of-speech tag for open-class words on the source side. For the rule above and a simple tag-set the pattern tracked by such an indicator function would be $d'\ A_1\ N\ A_2$. We require all reordering features to be conjoined with an indicator function of this type, ensuring that each corresponds to a separate optimization subproblem. We further split larger optimization subproblems, so that parameters for identical reordering features are in some cases estimated separately for different subsets of rules.

Morphological inflection provides motivation for another class of features not bound to surface representations. In this paper we explore a particularly simple example of this approach, adding features conjoined with indicator functions for Arabic lemmas to the lexical models in Arabic-English translation. This preserves decomposition of parameter estimation, with subproblems now associated with individual lemmas rather than words. Lemma-based features suggest another extension of the modeling framework. Instead of computing the sums in normalization factors over all English words aligned to a given Arabic token in the training data, we let the sum range over all English words aligned to Arabic words sharing its lemma. This also defines probabilities for Arabic words whose surface forms have not been observed in training, although we do not take advantage of estimates for out-of-vocabulary words in the experiments below.

3.5 Regularization

We apply ℓ_1 regularization (Ng, 2004; Gao et al., 2007) to make learning more robust to noise and control the effective dimensionality of the feature space by subtracting a weighted sum of absolute values of parameter weights from the log-likelihood of the training data

$$\mathbf{w}^* = \arg\max_{\mathbf{w}} LL(\mathbf{w}) - \sum_i C_i |w_i| \quad (6)$$

We optimize the objective using a variant of the orthant-wise limited-memory quasi-Newton algorithm proposed by Andrew & Gao (2007).[3] All values C_i are set to 1 in most of the experiments below, although we apply stronger regularization ($C_i = 3$) to reordering features. Tuning regularization tradeoffs individually for different feature types is an attractive option, but our experiments suggest that using cross-entropy on a held-out portion of training data for that purpose does not help performance. We leave investigation of the alternatives for future work.

4 Experiments

4.1 Data and methods

We apply the models to Arabic-English and Chinese-English translation, with training sets consisting of 108,268 and 1,017,930 sentence pairs, respectively.[4] All conditions use word alignments produced by sequential iterations of IBM model 1, HMM, and IBM model 4 in GIZA++ , followed by "diag-and" symmetrization (Koehn et al., 2003). Thresholds for phrase extraction and decoder pruning were set to values typical for the baseline system (Chiang, 2007). Unaligned words at the outer edges of rules or gaps were disallowed. A trigram language model with modified interpolated Kneser-Ney smoothing (Chen and Goodman, 1998) was trained by the SRILM toolkit on the Xinhua portion of the Gigaword corpus and the English side of the parallel training set. Evaluation was based on the BLEU score with 95% bootstrap confidence intervals for the score and difference between scores, calculated by scripts in version 11a of the NIST distribution. The 2002 NIST MT evaluation sets was used for development. The 2003, 2004, 2005, and 2006 sets were used for testing.

The decision rule was based on the standard log-linear interpolation of several models, with weights tuned by MERT on the development set (Och, 2003). The baseline consisted of the language model, two phrase translation models, two lexical models, and a brevity penalty. In the runs where generalized exponential models were used they replaced both of the baseline phrase translation models. The feature set used for exponential phrase models in the experiments included all the rules in the grammar and all aligned word pairs for lexical models. Elementary contextual features were based on Viterbi parses obtained from the Stanford parser. Word features included identities of word unigrams and bigrams adjacent to a given rule, possibly including rule words. Part-of-speech features included similar ngrams up to the length of 3 and the tags for rule tokens. These features were collected for training by a straightforward extension of rule extraction algorithms implemented in the baseline system for each possible location of ngrams with respect to the rule: namely, at the outer edges of the rule and at the edges of any gaps that it has. Our models also include a subset of contextual features formed by pairwise combinations of these elementary features. A final type of contextual features in these experiments was the sequence of the highest nodes in the parse tree that fill the span of the rule and the sequences that fill its gaps. We used an in-house Arabic tokenizer based on a Java implementation of Buckwalter's morphological analyzer and incorporating simple statistics from the Penn Arabic treebank, also extending it to

[3]Our implementation of the algorithm as a SciPy routine is available at `http://www.umiacs.umd.edu/~msubotin/owlqn.py`

[4]The Arabic-English data came from Arabic News Translation Text Part 1 (LDC2004T17), Arabic English Parallel News Text (LDC2004T18), and Arabic Treebank English Translation (LDC2005E46). Chinese-English data came from Xinhua Chinese English Parallel News Text Version 1 beta (LDC2002E18), Chinese Treebank English Parallel Corpus (LDC2003E07), Chinese English News Magazine Parallel Text (LDC2005T10), FBIS Multilanguage Texts (LDC2003E14), Chinese News Translation Text Part 1 (LDC2005T06), and the HKNews portion of Hong Kong Parallel Text (LDC2004T08). Some sentence pairs were not included in the training sets due to large length discrepancies.

perform lemmatization.

The total number of candidate features thus defined is very large, and we use a number of simple heuristics to reduce it prior to training. They are not essential to the estimates and were chosen so that the models could be trained in a few hours on a small cluster. With the exception of discarding all except the 10 most frequent target phrases observed with each source phrase,[5] which benefits performance, we expect that relaxing these restrictions would improve the score. These limitations included count-based thresholds on the frequency of contextual features included into the model, the frequency of rules and reordering patterns conjoined with other features, and the size of optimization subproblems to which contextual features are added. We don't conjoin contextual features to rules whose source phrase terminals are all punctuation symbols. For subproblems of size exceeding a certain threshold, we train on a subsample of available training instances. For the Chinese-English task we do not add reordering features to problems with low-entropy distributions of inversion and reordering patterns and discard rules with two non-terminals altogether if the entropy of their reordering patterns falls under a threshold. None of these restrictions were applied to the baselines. Finally, we solve only those optimization subproblems which include parameters needed in the development and training sets. This leads to a reduction of costs that is similar to phrase table filtering and likewise does not affect the solution. At decoding time all features for the translation models and their weights are accessed from a disk-mapped trie.

4.2 Results and discussion

The results are shown in tables 1 and 2. For both language pairs we had a choice between using a baseline that is computed in the same way as the other exponential models, with the exception of its use of relative frequency estimates and a baseline that incorporates averaged fractional counts for phrase models and lexical models, as used by Chiang (2007). For the sake of completeness we report both (though without performing statistical comparisons between

[5]This has prompted us to add an additional target-side token to lexical models, which subsumes the discarded items under a single category.

Condition	MT03	MT04	MT05	MT06
Rel. freq.	48.24	43.92	47.53	37.94
Frac.	48.34	45.68	47.95	39.41
Context	49.47*	45.65	48.76	39.49
+lex	**50.42***	46.07*	**49.66***	39.32
+lex+lemma	49.86*	**47.02***	49.29*	**40.81***

Table 1: Arabic-English translation, BLEU scores on testing. Conditions include two baselines: simple relative frequency (rel. freq.) and fractional estimates (frac.). Experimental conditions: contextual features in phrase models (context); same and contextual features in lexical models (+lex); same and lemma based features in lexical models (+lex+lemma). Stars mark statistically significant improvements over the fractional baseline which produced a higher score on the dev-test MT02 set than the other baseline (59.75 vs. 59.66).

Condition	MT03	MT04	MT05	MT06
Rel. freq.	32.62	27.53	30.50	22.78
Frac.	32.56	27.98	30.42	23.16
Context	33.16*	**28.35***	31.52*	**23.67***
+lex	**33.50***	28.14*	**31.98***	23.05
+lex+reord	33.12*	28.27*	31.73*	23.45*

Table 2: Chinese-English translation, BLEU scores on testing. Conditions include two baselines: simple relative frequency (rel. freq.) and fractional estimates (frac.). Experimental conditions: contextual features in phrase models (context); same and contextual features in lexical models (+lex); same and reordering features in phrase models (+lex+reord). Stars mark statistically significant improvements over the simple relative frequency baseline which produced a higher score on the dev-test MT02 set than the other baseline (33.62 vs. 33.53).

them). Statistical tests for experimental conditions were performed in comparison to the baseline which achieved higher score on the test-dev MT02 set: the fractional count baseline for Arabic-English and the simple relative count baseline for Chinese-English.

We test models with classifier solutions for phrase models alone and for phrase models together with lexical models in both language pairs. For Arabic-English translation we also experiment with adding features based on lemmas to lexical models, while for Chinese-English we add "reordering" features – features based on the ordering pattern of gaps for rules with two gaps and features based on ordering of gaps and words for rules with a single gap.

For both language pairs the results show consistent distinctions in behavior of different models between the test sets giving rise to generally higher scores (MT03 and MT05) and generally lower scores (MT04 and MT06). The fractional counts seem to be consistently more helpful for test sets with poorer coverage, although the reason for this is not immediately clear. For exponential models the two type of sets present two possible sources of difference. The lower-performing sets have poorer coverage in the training data, and they also may suffer from lower-quality annotation, since the training sets for both the translation models and the annotation tools are dominated by text in the same, newswire domain. Overall, the use of features based on surface forms is more beneficial for MT03 and MT05. Indeed, using lexical models with contextual features in addition to phrase models hurts performance on MT06 for Arabic-English and on both MT04 and MT06 for Chinese-English. In contrast, using features based on less specific representations is more beneficial on test sets with poorer coverage, while hurting performance on MT03 and MT05. This agrees with our intuitions and also suggests that the differences in coverage of training data for the translation models may be playing a more important role in these trends than coverage for annotation tools.

5 Conclusion

We have outlined a framework for translation modeling that synthesizes several recent advances in phrase-based machine translation and suggests many other ways to leverage sub-token representations of words as well as syntactic and morphological annotation tools, of which the experiments reported here explore only a small fraction. Indeed, the range and practicality of the available options is perhaps its most attractive feature. The inital results are promising and we are optimistic that continued exploration of this class of models will uncover even more effective uses.

Acknowledgments

I would like to thank David Chiang, Chris Dyer, Lise Getoor, Kevin Gimpel, Adam Lopez, Nitin Madnani, Smaranda Muresan, Noah Smith, Amy Weinberg and especially Philip Resnik for discussions relating to this work. I am also grateful to David Chiang for sharing source code of the Hiero translation system and to the two anonymous reviewers for their constructive comments.

References

Galen Andrew and Jianfeng Gao. 2007. Scalable training of L1-regularized log-linear models. In *Proc. ICML 2007*

Gökhan H. Bakır, Thomas Hofmann, Bernhard Schölkopf, Alexander J. Smola, Ben Taskar and S. V. N. Vishwanathan, eds. 2007. *Predicting Structured Data.* MIT Press.

Adam Berger, Stephen Della Pietra, and Vincent Della Pietra. 1996. A maximum entropy approach to natural language processing *Computational Linguistics*, 22(1).

Phil Blunsom, Trevor Cohn and Miles Osborne. 2008. Discriminative Synchronous Transduction for Statistical Machine Translation In *proc. ACL 2008.*

Marine Carpuat and Dekai Wu. 2007a. Improving Statistical Machine Translation using Word Sense Disambiguation In *Joint Conference on Empirical Methods in Natural Language Processing and Computational Natural Language Learning (EMNLP-CoNLL 2007)..*

Marine Carpuat and Dekai Wu. 2007b. How Phrase Sense Disambiguation outperforms Word Sense Disambiguation for Statistical Machine Translation. In *11th Conference on Theoretical and Methodological Issues in Machine Translation (TMI 2007).*

Yee Seng Chan, Hwee Tou Ng, and David Chiang. 2007. Word sense disambiguation improves statistical machine translation. In *Proc. ACL.*

Stanley F. Chen and Joshua T. Goodman. 1998. An Empirical Study of Smoothing Techniques for Language

Modeling. *Technical Report TR-10-98, Computer Science Group, Harvard University.*

David Chiang. 2007. Hierarchical phrase-based translation. *Computational Linguistics*, 33(2):201-228.

Corinna Cortes, Mehryar Mohri, and Jason Weston. 2007. A General Regression Framework for Learning String-to-String Mappings. In *Predicting Structured Data*. MIT Press.

Brooke Cowan, Ivona Kucerova, and Michael Collins. 2006. A Discriminative Model for Tree-to-Tree Translation. In *proceedings of EMNLP 2006.*

J. Gao, G. Andrew, M. Johnson and K. Toutanova 2007. A Comparative Study of Parameter Estimation Methods for Statistical Natural Language Processing. In *Proc. ACL 2007.*

Philipp Koehn, Franz Josef Och, and Daniel Marcu. 2003. Statistical Phrase-Based Translation. *Proceedings of the Human Language Technology Conference (HLT-NAACL 2003).*

P. Liang, Alexandre Bouchard-Cote, D. Klein and B. Taskar. 2006. An End-to-End Discriminative Approach to Machine Translation. In *Association for Computational Linguistics (ACL06).*

A. Y. Ng. 2004. Feature selection, L1 vs. L2 regularization, and rotational invariance In *Proceedings of the Twenty-first International Conference on Machine Learning*

Franz Josef Och. 2003. Minimum Error Rate Training for Statistical Machine Translation. In *ACL 2003: Proc. of the 41st Annual Meeting of the Association for Computational Linguistics.*

F. Pérez-Cruz, Z. Ghahramani and M. Pontil. 2007. Kernel Conditional Graphical Models In *Predicting Structured Data*. MIT Press.

Michael Subotin. 2008. Exponential models for machine translation. *Generals paper, Department of Linguistics, University of Maryland.*

Charles Sutton and Andrew McCallum. 2005. Piecewise training for undirected models. In *Conference on Uncertainty in Artificial Intelligence (UAI).*

Charles Sutton and Tom Minka. 2006. Local Training and Belief Propagation. *Microsoft Research Technical Report TR-2006-121..*

Christoph Tillmann and Tong Zhang 2006. A Discriminative Global Training Algorithm for Statistical MT. In *Association for Computational Linguistics (ACL06).*

Joseph Turian, Benjamin Wellington, and I. Dan Melamed 2006. Scalable Discriminative Learning for Natural Language Parsing and Translation In *Proceedings of the 20th Annual Conference on Neural Information Processing Systems (NIPS).*

Zhuoran Wang, John Shawe-Taylor, and Sandor Szedmak 2007. Kernel Regression Based Machine Translation. In *Proceedings of NAACL HLT.*

D. Xiong, Q. Liu, and S. Lin. 2006. Maximum entropy based phrase reordering model for statistical machine translation. In *Proceedings of the 21st international Conference on Computational Linguistics and the 44th Annual Meeting of the ACL.*

A Rule-Driven Dynamic Programming Decoder for Statistical MT

Christoph Tillmann
IBM T.J. Watson Research Center
Yorktown Heights, N.Y. 10598
ctill@us.ibm.com

Abstract

The paper presents an extension of a dynamic programming (DP) decoder for phrase-based SMT (Koehn, 2004; Och and Ney, 2004) that tightly integrates POS-based re-order rules (Crego and Marino, 2006) into a left-to-right beam-search algorithm, rather than handling them in a pre-processing or re-order graph generation step. The novel decoding algorithm can handle tens of thousands of rules efficiently. An improvement over a standard phrase-based decoder is shown on an Arabic-English translation task with respect to translation accuracy and speed for large re-order window sizes.

1 Introduction

The paper presents an extension of a dynamic programming (DP) decoder for phrase-based SMT (Koehn, 2004; Och and Ney, 2004) where POS-based re-order rules (Crego and Marino, 2006) are tightly integrated into a left-to-right run over the input sentence. In the literature, re-order rules are applied to the source and/or target sentence as a pre-processing step (Xia and McCord, 2004; Collins et al., 2005; Wang et al., 2007) where the rules can be applied on both training and test data. Another way of incorporating re-order rules is via extended monotone search graphs (Crego and Marino, 2006) or lattices (Zhang et al., 2007; Paulik et al., 2007). This paper presents a way of handling POS-based re-order rules as an edge generation process: the POS-based re-order rules are tightly integrated into a left to right beam search decoder in a way that 29 000 rules which may overlap in an arbitrary way (but not recursively) are handled efficiently. Example rules which are used to control the novel DP-based decoder are shown in Table 1, where each POS sequence is associated with possibly several permutations π. In order to apply the rules, the input sentences are POS-tagged. If a POS sequence of a rule matches some identical POS sequence in the input sentence the corresponding words are re-ordered according to π. The contributions of this paper are as follows: 1) The novel DP decoder can handle tens of thousands of POS-based rules efficiently rather than a few dozen rules as is typically reported in the SMT literature by tightly integrating them into a beam search algorithm. As a result phrase re-ordering with a large distortion window can be carried out efficiently and reliably. 2) The current rule-driven decoder is a first step towards including more complex rules, i.e. syntax-based rules as in (Wang et al., 2007) or chunk rules as in (Zhang et al., 2007) using a decoding algorithm that is conceptually similar to an Earley-style parser (Earley, 1970). More generally, 'rule-driven' decoding is tightly linked to standard phrase-based decoding. In future, the edge generation technique presented in this paper might be extended to handle hierarchical rules (Chiang, 2007) in a simple left-to-right beam search decoder.

In the next section, we briefly summarize the baseline decoder. Section 3 shows the novel rule-driven DP decoder. Section 4 shows how the current decoder is related to both DP-based decoding algorithms in speech recognition and parsing. Finally,

Proceedings of the Second ACL Workshop on Syntax and Structure in Statistical Translation (SSST-2), pages 37–45,
ACL-08: HLT, Columbus, Ohio, USA, June 2008.

Table 1: A list of 28 878 reorder rules sorted according to the rule occurrence count $N(r)$ is used in this paper. For each POS sequence the corresponding permutation π is shown. Rule ID is the ordinal number of a rule in the sorted list. The maximum rule length that can be handled efficiently is surprisingly long: about 20 words.

Rule ID r	POS sequence		π	$N(r)$
1	DET NOUN DET ADJ	$\rightarrow$	2 3 0 1	4 421
2	DET NOUN NSUFF-FEM-SG DET ADJ NSUFF-FEM-SG	$\rightarrow$	3 4 5 0 1 2	2 257
⋮	⋮		⋮	
3 000	NOUN CASE-INDEF-ACC ADJ NSUFF-FEM-SG CONJ ADJ NSUFF-FEM-SG	$\rightarrow$	2 3 4 5 6 0 1	6
⋮	⋮		⋮	
28 878	PREP DET NOUN DET ADJ PREP NOUN-PROP ADJ NSUFF-MASC-SG-ACC-INDEF CONJ IV3MS IV IVSUFF-DO:3FS	$\rightarrow$	0 1 2 7 8 3 4 9 10 11 12 5 6	2

Section 5 shows experimental results.

2 Baseline DP Decoder

The translation model used in this paper is a phrase-based model (Koehn et al., 2003), where the translation units are so-called blocks: a block b is a pair consisting of a source phrase s and a target phrase t which are translations of each other. The expression block is used here to emphasize that pairs of phrases (especially longer phrases) tend to form closely linked units in such a way that the translation process can be formalized as a block segmentation process (Nagata et al., 2006; Tillmann and Zhang, 2007). Here, the input sentence is segmented from left to right while simultaneously generating the target sentence, one block at a time. In practice, phrase-based or block-based translation models which largely monotone decoding algorithms obtain close to state-of-the-art performance by using skip and window-based restrictions to reduce the search space (Berger et al., 1996). During decoding, we maximize the score $s_w(b_1^n)$ of a phrase-pair sequence $b_1^n = (s_i, t_i)_1^n$:

$$s_w(b_1^n) \;=\; \sum_{i=1}^{n} w^T \cdot f(b_i, b_{i-1}), \qquad (1)$$

where b_i is a block, b_{i-1} is its predecessor block, and $f(b_i, b_{i-1})$ is a 8-dimensional feature vector where the features are derived from some probabilistic models: language model, translation model, and distortion model probabilities. n is the number of blocks in the translation and the weight vector w is trained in a way as to maximize the decoder **BLEU** score on some training data using an on-line algorithm (Tillmann and Zhang, 2008). The decoder that carries out the optimization in Eq. 1 is similar to a standard phrase-based decoder (Koehn, 2004; Och and Ney, 2004), where states are tuples of the following type:

$$[\, \mathcal{C}\, ;\; [i,j]\,], \qquad (2)$$

where $\mathcal{C}$ is the so-called coverage vector that keeps track of the already processed source position, $[i,j]$ is the source interval covered by the last source phrase match. In comparison, (Koehn, 2004) uses only the position of the final word of the last source phrase translated. Since we are using the distortion model in (Al-Onaizan and Papineni, 2006) the entire last source phrase interval needs to be stored. Hypothesis score and language model history are omitted for brevity reasons. The states are stored in lists or stacks and DP recombination is used to reduce the size of the search space while extending states.

The algorithm described in this paper uses an intermediate data structure called an *edge* that represents a source phrase together with a target phrase that is one of its possible translation. Formally, we define:

$$[\, [i,j]\, ,\; t_1^N\,], \qquad (3)$$

where t_1^N is the target phrase linked to the source phrase $s_i, \cdots, s_j$. The edges are stored in a so-called *chart*. For each input interval that is matched by some source phrase in the block set, a list of possible target phrase translations is stored in the chart. Here, *simple* edges as in Eq. 3 are used to generate so-called rule edges that are defined later in the paper. A similar data structure corresponding to an edge is called *translation option* in (Koehn, 2004). While the edge generation potentially slows down the overall decoding process, for the baseline de-

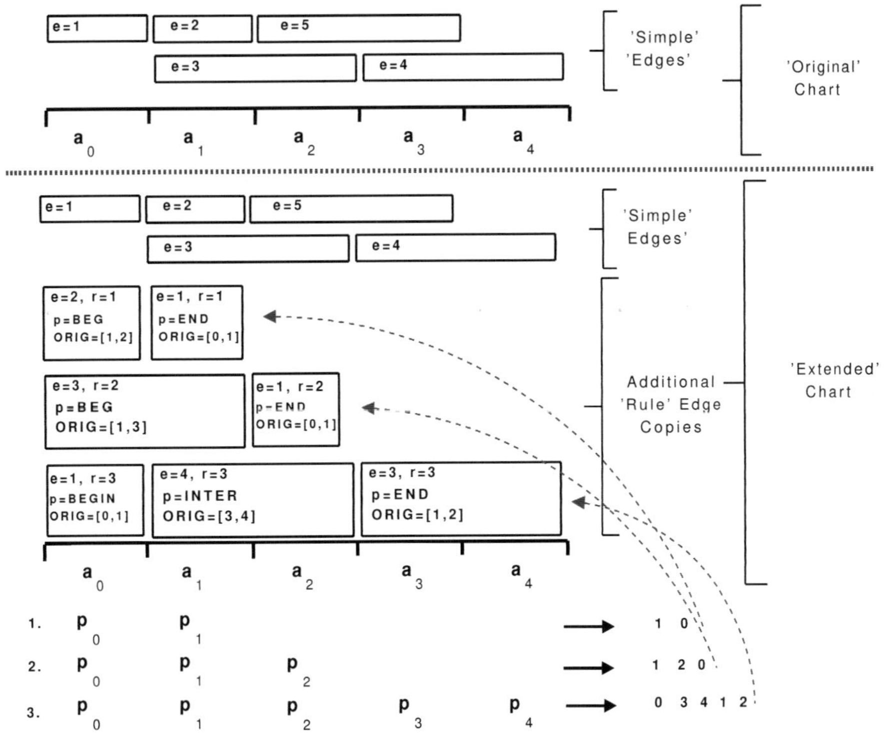

Figure 1: Addition of rule edges to a chart containing 5 simple edges (some rule edges are not shown). The simple edges remain in the chart after the rule edges have been added: they are used to carry out monotone translations.

coder generating all the simple edges takes less than 0.3 % of the overall decoding time.

3 DP-Search with Rules

This section explains the handling of the re-order rules as an edge generation process. Assuming a monotone translation, for the baseline DP decoder (Koehn, 2004) each edge ending at position j can be continued by any edge starting at position $j+1$, i.e. the simple edges are fully connected with respect to their start and ending positions. For the rule-driven decoder, all the re-ordering is handled by generating additional edges which are 'copies' of the simple edges in each rule context in which they occur. Here, a rule edge copy ending at position j is not fully connected with all other edges starting at position $j+1$. Once a rule edge copy for a particular rule id r has been processed that edge can be continued only by an edge copy for the same rule until the end of the rule has been reached. To formalize the approach, the search state definition in Eq. 2 is modified as follows:

$$[\ s\ ;\ [i,j]\ ,r\ ,\ s_r\ ,\ e \in \{\textbf{false}, \textbf{true}\}\ ] \qquad (4)$$

Here, the coverage vector C is replaced by a single number s: a monotone search is carried out and all the source positions up to position s (including s) are covered. $[i,j]$ is the coverage interval for the last source phrase translated (the same as in Eq. 2). r is the rule identifier, i.e. a rule position in the list in Table 1. s_r is the starting position for the rule match of rule r in the input sentence, and e is a flag that indicates whether the hypothesis h has covered the entire span of rule r yet. The search starts with the following initial state:

$$[\ -1\ ;\ [-1,-1]\ ,-1\ ,\ -1\ ,\ e = \textbf{true}\ ], \qquad (5)$$

where the starting positions s, s_r, and the coverage interval $[i,j]$ are all initialized with -1, a virtual source position to the left of the uncovered source input. Throughout the search, a rule id of -1 indicates that no rule is currently applied for that hypothesis, i.e. a contiguous source interval to the left of s is covered.

States are extended by finding matching edges and the generation of these edges is illustrated in Fig. 1 for the use of 3 overlapping rules on a source segment of 5 words $a_0, \cdots, a_4$ [1]. Edges are shown as rectangles where the number on the left inside the box corresponds to the enumeration of the simple edges. In the top half of the picture the simple edges which correspond to 5 phrase-to-phrase translations are shown. In the bottom half all the edges after the rule edge extension are shown (including simple *and* rule edges). A rule edge contains additional components: the rule id r, a relative edge position p (explained below), and the original source interval of a rule edge before it has been re-ordered. A rule edge is generated from a simple edge via a re-order rule application: the newly generated edges are added into the chart as shown in the lower half of Figure 1. Here, rule 1 and 2 generate two new edges and rule 3 generates three new edges that are added into the chart at their new re-ordered positions, e.g. copies of edge 1 are added for the rule id $r = 1$ at start position 2, for rule $r = 2$ at start position 3, and for rule $r = 3$ at start position 0. Even if an edge copy is added at the same position as the original edge a new copy is needed. The three rules correspond to matching POS sequences, i.e. the Arabic input sentence has been POS tagged and a POS p_j has been assigned to each Arabic word a_j. The same POS sequence might generate several different permutations which is not shown here.

More formally, the edge generation process is carried out as follows. First, for each source interval $[k, l]$ all the matching phrase pairs are found and added into the chart as simple edges. In a second run over the input sentence for each source interval $[k, l]$ all matching POS sequences are computed and the corresponding source words $a_k, \cdots, a_l$ are re-ordered according to the rule permutation. On the re-ordered word sequence phrase matches are computed only for those source phrases that already occurred in the original (un-reordered) source sentence. Both edge generation steps together still take less than 1 % of the overall decoding time as shown in Section 5: most of the decoding time is needed to access the translation and the language model probabilities when extending partial decoder hypotheses [2]. Typically rule matches are much longer than edge matches where several simple edges are needed to cover the entire rule interval, i.e. three edges for rule $r = 3$ in Fig. 1. As the edge copies corresponding to the same rule must be processed in sequence they are assigned one out of three possible positions p:

- BEG: Edge copy matches at the begin of rule match.
- INTER: Edge copy lies within rule match interval.
- END: Edge copy matches at the end of rule match.

Formally, the rule edges in Fig. 1 are defined as follows, where a rule edge includes all the components of a simple edge:

$$\Big[\, [i,j]\ ,\ t_1^N\ ,\ r, p, [\pi(i), \pi(j)] \,\Big], \qquad (6)$$

where r is the rule id and p is the relative edge position. $[\pi(i), \pi(j)]$ is the original coverage interval where the edge matched before being re-ordered. The original interval is not a necessary component of the rule-driven algorithm but it makes a direct comparison with the window-based decoder straightforward as explained below. The rule edge definition for a rule r that matches at position s_r is slightly simplified: the processing interval is actually $[s_r + i, s_r + j]$ and the original interval is $[s_r + \pi(i), s_r + \pi(j)]$. For simplicity reasons, the offset s_r is omitted in Fig 1. Using the original interval has the following advantage: as the edges are processed from left-to-right and the re-ordering is controlled by the rules the translation score computation is based on the original source interval $[\pi(i), \pi(j)]$ and the monotone processing is based on the matching interval $[i, j]$. For the rule-driven decoder it looks like the re-ordering is carried out like in a regular decoder with a window-based re-ordering restriction, but the rule-induced window can be large, i.e. up to 15 source word positions. In particular a distortion model can be applied when using the

[1] Rule edges and simple edges may overlap arbitrarily, but the final translation constitutes a non-overlapping boundary sequence.

[2] Strictly speaking, the edge generation constitutes two additional runs over the input sentence. In future, the rule edges can be computed 'on demand' for each input position j resulting in an even stricter implementation of the beam search concept.

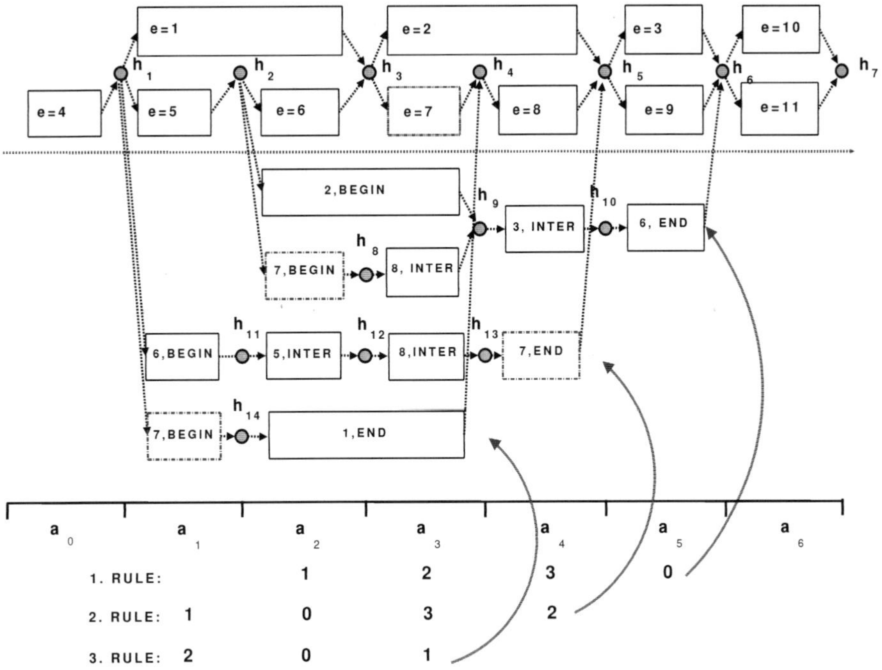

Figure 2: Search lattice for the rule-driven decoder. The gray circles indicated partial hypotheses. An hypothesis is expanded by applying an edge. DP recombination is used to restrict the search space throughout the rule lattice.

re-order rules. Additionally, rule-based probabilities can be used as well. This concept allows to directly compare a window-based decoder and the current rule based decoder in Section 5.

The search space for the rule-driven decoder is illustrated in Fig. 2. The gray shaded circles represent translation hypotheses according to Eq. 4. A translation hypothesis h_1 is extended by an edge which covers some uncovered portion of the input sentence to produce a new hypothesis h_2. The decoder searches monotonically through the entire chart of edges, and word re-ordering is possible only through the use of rule edges. The top half of the picture shows the way simple edges contribute to the search process: they are used to carry out a monotone translation. The dashed arrows indicate that hypotheses can be *recombined*: when extending hypothesis h_3 by edge $e = 2$ and hypothesis h_4 by edge $e = 8$ only a single hypothesis h_5 is kept as the history of edge extensions can be ignored for future decoder decisions with respect to the uncovered source positions. Here, the distortion model and the language model history are ignored for illustration purposes. As it can be seen in Fig. 2, the rule edge generation step has created 3 copies of the simple edge $e = 7$, which are marked by a dashed borderline. Hypotheses covering the same input may not be merged, i.e. hypotheses h_9 and h_{13} for rules $r = 1$ and $r = 2$ have to be kept separate from the hypothesis h_4. But state merging may occur for states generated by rule edges for the same rule r, i.e. rule $r = 1$ and state h_9.

Since rule edges have to be processed in a sequential order, looking up those that can extend a given hypothesis h is more complicated than a phrase translation look-up in a regular decoder. Given the search state definition in Eq. 4, for a given rule id r and coverage position s we have to be able to look-up all possible edge extensions efficiently. This is implemented by storing two lists:

1. For each source position j a list of possible 'starting' edges: these are all the simple edges plus all rule edges with relative edge position $p =$ BEG. This list is used to expand hypotheses according to the definition in Eq. 4 where the rule flag $e =$ **true**, i.e. the search has finished covering an entire rule interval.

2. The second list is for continuing edges ($p =$ INTER or $p =$ END). For each rule id r, rule

start position s_r and source position j a list of rule edges has to be stored that can continue an already started rule coverage. This list is used to expand hypotheses for which the rule flag e is $e =$ **false**, i.e. the hypothesis has not yet finished covering the current rule interval, e.g. the hypotheses h_9 and h_{11} in Fig. 2.

The two lists are computed by a single run over the chart after all chart edges have been generated and before the search is carried out (the CPU time to generate these lists is included in the edge generation CPU time reported in Section 5). The two lists are used to find the successor edges for each hypothesis h that corresponds to a rule r efficiently: only a small fraction of the chart edges starting at position j needs to be retrieved for an extension. The rule start position s_r has to be included for the second list: it is possible that the same rule r matches the input sentences for two intervals $[i, j]$ and $[i', j']$ which overlap. This results in an invalid search state configuration. Based on the two lists a monotone search is carried out over the extended rule edge set which implicitly generates a reordering lattice as in similar approaches (Crego and Marino, 2006; Zhang et al., 2007). But because the handling of the edges is tightly integrated into the beam search algorithm by applying the same beam thresholds it potentially handles 10's of thousands of rules efficiently.

4 DP Search

The DP decoder described in the previous section bears some resemblance with search algorithms for large vocabulary speech recognition. For example, (Jelinek, 1998) presents a Viterbi decoder that searches a composite trellis consisting of smaller HMM acoustic trellises that are combined with language model states in the case a trigram language model. Multiple 'copies' of the same acoustic sub models are incorporated into the overall trellis. The highest probability word sequences is obtained using a Viterbi shortest path finding algorithm in a possibly huge composite HMM (cf. Fig. 5.3 of (Jelinek, 1998)). In comparison, in this paper the edge 'copies' are used to generate hypotheses that are hypotheses 'copies' of the same phrase match, e.g. in Fig. 2 the states h_4, h_8, and h_{14} all result from covering the same simple edge e_7 as the most recent phrase match. The states form a potentially huge lattice as shown in Fig. 2. Similarly, (Ortmanns and Ney, 2000) presents a DP search algorithm where the interdependent decisions between non-linear time alignment, word boundary detection, and word identification (the pronunciation lexicon is organized efficiently as a lexical tree) are all carried out by searching a shortest path trough a possibly huge composite trellis or HMM. The similarity between those speech recognition algorithms and the current rule decoder derives from the following observation: the use of a language model in speech recognition introduces a coupling between adjacent acoustic word models. Similarly, a rule match which typically spans several source phrase matches introduces a coupling between adjacent simple edges. Viewed in this way, the handling of copies is a technique of incorporating higher-level knowledge sources into a simple one-step search process: either by processing acoustic models in the context of a language model or by processing simple edges in the context of bigger re-ordering units, which exploit a richer linguistic context.

The Earley parser in the presentation (Jurafsky and Martin, 2000) also uses the notion of **edges** which represent partial constituents derived in the parsing process. These constituents are interpreted as edges in a directed acyclic graph (DAG) which represents the set of all sub parse trees considered. This paper uses the notion of **edges** as well following (Tillmann, 2006) where phrase-based decoding is also linked to a DAG path finding problem. Since the re-order rules are not applied recursively, the rule-driven algorithm can be linked to an Earley parser where parsing is done with a linear grammar (for a definition of linear grammar see (Harrison, 1978)). A formal analysis of the rule-driven decoder might be important because of the following consideration: in phrase-based machine translation the target sentence is generated from left-to-right by concatenating target phrases linked to source phrases that cover some source positions. Here, a coverage vector is typically used to ensure that each source position is covered a limited number of times (typically once). Including a coverage vector $\mathcal{C}$ into the search state definition results in an inherently exponential complexity: for an input sentence of length J there are 2^J coverage vectors (Koehn, 2004). On

Table 2: Translation results on the MT06 data. w is the distortion limit.

		words / sec	generation [%]	**BLEU**	**PREC**	**TER**
Baseline decoder	$w = 0$	171.6	1.90	34.6	35.2	65.3
	$w = 2$	25.4	0.29	36.6	37.7	63.5
	$w = 5$	8.2	0.10	35.0	36.1	65.1
Rule decoder	$N(r) \geq 2$	9.1	0.75	37.1	38.2	63.5
($w = 15$)	$N(r) \geq 5$	10.5	0.43	37.2	38.2	63.5

the contrary, the search state definition in Eq. 4 explicitly avoids the use of a coverage vector resulting in an essentially linear time decoding algorithm (Section 5 reports the size of the the extended search graph in terms of number of edges and shows that the number of permutations per POS sequence is less than 2 on average). The rule-driven algorithm might be formally *correct* in the following sense. A phrase-based decoder has to generate a phrase alignment where each source position needs to be covered by exactly one source phrase. The rule-based decoder achieves this by *local* computation only: 1) no coverage vector is used, 2) the rule edge generation is local to each individual rule, i.e. looking only at the span of that rule, and 3) rules whose application spans overlap arbitrarily (but not recursively) are handled correctly. In future, a formal correctness proof might be given.

5 Experimental Results

We test the novel edge generation algorithm on a standard Arabic-to-English translation tasks: the MT06 Arabic-English DARPA evaluation set consisting of 1 529 sentences with 58 331 Arabic words and 4 English reference translations . The translation model is defined in Eq. 1 where 8 probabilistic features (language, translation,distortion model) are used. The distortion model is similar to (Al-Onaizan and Papineni, 2006). An on-line algorithm similar to (Tillmann and Zhang, 2008) is used to train the weight vector w. The decoder uses a 5-gram language model , and the phrase table consists of about 3.2 million phrase pairs. The phrase table as well as the probabilistic features are trained on a much larger training data consisting of 3.8 million sentences. Translation results are given in terms of the automatic **BLEU** evaluation metric (Papineni et al., 2002) as well as the **TER** metric (Snover et al., 2006).

Our baseline decoder is similar to (Koehn, 2004; Moore and Quirk, 2007). The goal of the current paper is not to demonstrate an improvement in decoding speed but show the validity of the rule edge generation algorithm. While the baseline and the rule-driven decoder are compared with respect to speed, they are both run with conservatively large beam thresholds, e.g. a beam limit of 500 hypotheses and a beam threshold of 7.5 (logarithmic scale) per source position j. The baseline decoder and the rule decoder use only 2 stacks to carry out the search (rather than a stack for each source position) (Tillmann, 2006). No rest-cost estimation is employed. For the results in line 2 the number of phrase 'holes' n in the coverage vector for a left to right traversal of the input sentence is restricted using a typical skip-based decoder (Berger et al., 1996). Up to 2 phrases can be skipped. Additionally, the phrase re-ordering is restricted to take place within a given window size w. The $28,878$ rules used in this paper are obtained from 14 989 manually aligned Arabic-English sentences where the Arabic sentences have been segmented and POS tagged . The rule selection procedure is similar to the one used in (Crego and Marino, 2006) and rules are extracted that occur at least twice. The rule-based re-ordering uses an additional probabilistic feature which is derived from the rule unigram count $N(r)$ shown in Table. 1: $p(r) = \frac{N(r)}{\sum_{r'} N(r')}$. The average number of POS sequence matches per input sentence is 34.9 where the average number of permutations that generate edges is 57.7. The average number of simple edges i.e. phrase pairs per input sentence is 751.1. For the rule-based decoder the average number of edges is 3187.8 which includes the simple edges.

Table 2 presents results that compare the baseline decoder with the rule-driven decoder in terms of translation performance and decoding speed. The second column shows the distortion limit used by the two decoders. For the rule-based decoder a maximum distortion limit w is implemented by filtering out all the rule matches where the size of the rule in terms of number of POS symbols is greater than w, i.e. the rule edges are processed monotonically but a monotone rule edge sequence for the same rule id may not span more than w source positions. The third column shows the translation speed in terms of words per second. The fourth column shows the percentage of CPU time needed for the edge generation (including both simple and rule edges). The final three columns report translation results in terms of **BLEU** , **BLEU** precision score (**PREC**), and **TER**. The rule-based reordering restriction obtains the best translation scores on the MT06 data: a **BLEU** score of 37.2 compared to a **BLEU** score of 36.6 for the baseline decoder. The statistical significance interval is rather large: 2.9 % on this test set as text from various genres is included. Additional visual evaluation on the dev set data shows that some successful phrase reordering is carried out by the rule decoder which is not handled correctly by the baseline decoder. As can be seen from the results reducing the number of rules by filtering all rules that occur at least 5 times (about 10 000 rules) slightly improves translation performance from 37.1 to 37.2. The edge generation accounts for only a small fraction of the overall decoding time. Fig. 3 and Fig. 4 demonstrate additional advantages when using the rule-based decoder. Fig. 3 shows the translation **BLEU** score as a function of the distortion limit window w. The **BLEU** score actually decreases for the baseline decoder as the size w is increased. The optimal window size is surprisingly small: $w = 2$. A similar behavior is also reported in (Moore and Quirk, 2007) where $w = 5$ is used . For the rule-driven decoder however the **BLEU** score does not decrease for large w: the rules restrict the local re-ordering in the context of potentially very long POS sequences which makes the re-ordering more reliable. Fig. 4 which shows the decoding speed as a function of the window size w demonstrates that the rule-based decoder actually runs faster than the baseline decoder for window sizes $w \geq 5$.

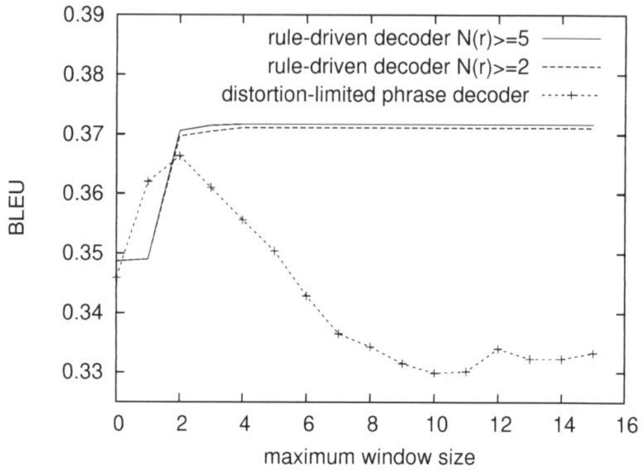

Figure 3: **BLEU** score as a function of window size w.

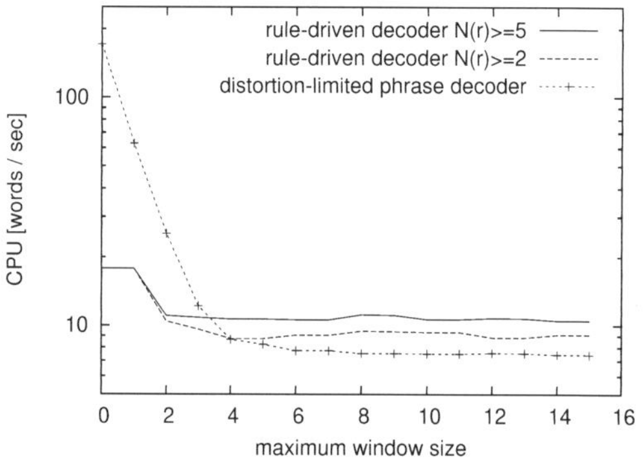

Figure 4: Decoding speed as a function of window size w.

6 Discussion and Future Work

The handling of the re-order rules is most similar to work in (Crego and Marino, 2006) where the rules are used to create re-order lattices. To make this feasible, the rules have been vigorously filtered in (Crego and Marino, 2006): only about 30 rules are used in their experiments. On the contrary, the current approach tightly integrates the re-order rules into a phrase-based decoder such that 29 000 rules can be handled efficiently. In future work our novel approach might allow to make use of lexicalized re-order rules as in (Xia and McCord, 2004) or syntactic rules as in (Wang et al., 2007).

7 Acknowledgment

This work was supported by the DARPA GALE project under the contract number HR0011-06-2-00001. The authors would like to thank the anonymous reviewers for their detailed criticism.

References

Yaser Al-Onaizan and Kishore Papineni. 2006. Distortion Models for Statistical Machine Translation. In *Proceedings of ACL-COLING'06*, pages 529–536, Sydney, Australia, July.

Adam L. Berger, Peter F. Brown, Stephen A. Della Pietra, Vincent J. Della Pietra, Andrew S. Kehler, and Robert L. Mercer. 1996. Language Translation Apparatus and Method of Using Context-Based Translation Models. *United States Patent, Patent Number 5510981*, April.

David Chiang. 2007. Hierarchical Machine Translation. *Computational Linguistics*, 33(2):201–228.

Michael Collins, Philipp Koehn, and Ivona Kucerova. 2005. Clause restructuring for statistical machine translation. In *Proc. of ACL'05*, pages 531–540, Ann Arbor, Michigan, June. Association for Computational Linguistics.

J.M. Crego and José B. Marino. 2006. Integration of POStag-based Source Reordering into SMT Decoding by an Extended Search Graph. In *Proc. of AMTA06*, pages 29–36, Cambridge, MA, August.

Jay Earley. 1970. An Efficient Context-Free Parsing Algorithm. *Communications of the ACM*, 13(2):94–102.

Michael A. Harrison. 1978. *Introduction to Formal Language Theory*. Addison Wesley.

Fred Jelinek. 1998. *Statistical Methods for Speech Recognition*. The MIT Press, Cambridge, MA.

Daniel Jurafsky and James H. Martin. 2000. *Speech and Language Processing*. Prentice Hall.

Philipp Koehn, Franz J. Och, and Daniel Marcu. 2003. Statistical phrase-based translation. In *HLT-NAACL'03: Main Proceedings*, pages 127–133, Edmonton, Alberta, Canada, May 27 - June 1.

Philipp Koehn. 2004. Pharaoh: a Beam Search Decoder for Phrase-Based Statistical Machine Translation Models. In *Proceedings of AMTA'04*, Washington DC, September-October.

Robet C. Moore and Chris Quirk. 2007. Faster Beam-search Decoding for Phrasal SMT. *Proc. of the MT Summit XI*, pages 321–327, September.

Masaaki Nagata, Kuniko Saito, Kazuhide Yamamoto, and Kazuteru Ohashi. 2006. A Clustered Global Phrase Reordering Model for Statistical Machine Translation. In *Proceedings of ACL-COLING'06*, pages 713–720, Sydney, Australia, July.

Franz-Josef Och and Hermann Ney. 2004. The Alignment Template Approach to Statistical Machine Translation. *Computational Linguistics*, 30(4):417–450.

Stefan Ortmanns and Hermann Ney. 2000. Progress in Dynamic Programming Search for LVCSR. *Proc. of the IEEE*, 88(8):1224–1240.

Kishore Papineni, Salim Roukos, Todd Ward, and Wei-Jing Zhu. 2002. BLEU: A Method for Automatic Evaluation of Machine Translation. In *Proc. of ACL'02*, pages 311–318, Philadelphia, PA, July.

Matthias Paulik, Kay Rottmann, Jan Niehues, Silja Hildebrand, and Stephan Vogel. 2007. The ISL Phrase-Based MT System for the 2007 ACL Workshop on SMT. *In Proc. of the ACL 2007 Second Workshop on SMT*, June.

Matthew Snover, Bonnie Dorr, Richard Schwartz, Linnea Micciulla, and John Makhoul. 2006. A Study of Translation Edit Rate with Targeted Human Annotation. In *Proc. of AMTA 2006*, Boston,MA.

Christoph Tillmann and Tong Zhang. 2007. A Block Bigram Prediction Model for Statistical Machine Translation. *ACM-TSLP*, 4(6):1–31, July.

Christoph Tillmann and Tong Zhang. 2008. An Online Relevant Set Algorithm for Statistical Machine Translation. *Accepted for publication in IEEE Transaction on Audio, Speech, and Language Processing.*

Christoph Tillmann. 2006. Efficient Dynamic Programming Search Algorithms for Phrase-based SMT. In *Proceedings of the Workshop CHPSLP at HLT'06*, pages 9–16, New York City, NY, June.

Chao Wang, Michael Collins, and Philipp Koehn. 2007. Chinese Syntactic reordering for statistical machine translation. In *Proc. of EMNLP-CoNLL'07*, pages 737–745, Prague, Czech Republic, July.

Fei Xia and Michael McCord. 2004. Improving a statistical mt system with automatically learned rewrite patterns. In *Proc. of Coling 2004*, pages 508–514, Geneva, Switzerland, Aug 23–Aug 27. COLING.

Yuqi Zhang, Richard Zens, and Hermann Ney. 2007. Chunk-level Reordering of Source Language Sentences with Automatically Learned Rules for Statistical Machine Translation. In *Proc. of SSST, NAACL-HLT'07 / AMTA Workshop*, pages 1–8, Rochester, NY, April.

Syntactic Reordering Integrated with Phrase-based SMT

Jakob Elming
Computational Linguistics
Copenhagen Business School
jel.isv@cbs.dk

Abstract

We present a novel approach to word reordering which successfully integrates syntactic structural knowledge with phrase-based SMT. This is done by constructing a lattice of alternatives based on automatically learned probabilistic syntactic rules. In decoding, the alternatives are scored based on the output word order, not the order of the input. Unlike previous approaches, this makes it possible to successfully integrate syntactic reordering with phrase-based SMT. On an English-Danish task, we achieve an absolute improvement in translation quality of 1.1 % BLEU. Manual evaluation supports the claim that the present approach is significantly superior to previous approaches.

1 Introduction

The emergence of phrase-based statistical machine translation (PSMT) (Koehn et al., 2003) has been one of the major developments in statistical approaches to translation. Allowing translation of word sequences (phrases) instead of single words provides SMT with a robustness in word selection and local word reordering.

PSMT has two means of reordering the words. Either a phrase pair has been learned where the target word order differs from the source (phrase internal reordering), or distance penalized orderings of target phrases are attempted in decoding (phrase external reordering). The first solution is strong, the second is weak.

The second solution is necessary for reorderings within a previously unseen sequence or over distances greater than the maximal phrase length. In this case, the system in essence relies on the target side language model to get the correct word order. The choice is made without knowing what the source is. Basically, it is a bias against phrase external reordering.

It seems clear that reordering often depends on higher level linguistic information, which is absent from PSMT. In recent work, there has been some progress towards integrating syntactic information with the statistical approach to reordering. In works such as (Xia and McCord, 2004; Collins et al., 2005; Wang et al., 2007; Habash, 2007), reordering decisions are done "deterministically", thus placing these decisions outside the actual PSMT system by learning to translate from a reordered source language. (Crego and Mariño, 2007; Zhang et al., 2007; Li et al., 2007) are more in the spirit of PSMT, in that multiple reorderings are presented to the PSMT system as (possibly weighted) options.

Still, there remains a basic conflict between the syntactic reordering rules and the PSMT system: one that is most likely due to the discrepancy between the translation units (phrases) and units of the linguistic rules, as (Zhang et al., 2007) point out.

In this paper, we proceed in the spirit of the non-deterministic approaches by providing the decoder with multiple source reorderings. But instead of scoring the input word order, we score the order of the output. By doing this, we avoid the integration problems of previous approaches.

It should be noted that even though the experiments are conducted within a source reordering approach, this scoring is also compatible with other ap-

Proceedings of the Second ACL Workshop on Syntax and Structure in Statistical Translation (SSST-2), pages 46–54,
ACL-08: HLT, Columbus, Ohio, USA, June 2008.

proach. We will, however, not look further into this possiblity in the present paper.

In addition, we automatically learn reordering rules based on several levels of linguistic information from word form to subordination and syntactic structure to produce reordering rules that are not restricted to operations on syntactic tree structure nodes.

In the next section, we discuss and contrast related work. Section 3 describes aspects of English and Danish structure that are relevant to reordering. Section 4 describes the automatic induction of reordering rules and its integration in PSMT. In section 5, we describe the SMT system used in the experiments. Section 6 evaluates and discusses the present approach.

2 Related Work

While several recent authors have achieved positive results, it has been difficult to integrate syntactic information while retaining the strengths of the statistical approach.

Several approaches do deterministic reordering. These do not integrate the reordering in the PSMT system; instead they place it outside the system by first reordering the source language, and then having a PSMT system translate from reordered source language to target language. (Collins et al., 2005; Wang et al., 2007) do this using manually created rules, and (Xia and McCord, 2004) and (Habash, 2007) use automatically extracted rules. All use rules extracted from syntactic parses.

As mentioned by (Al-Onaizan and Papineni, 2006), it can be problematic that these deterministic choices are beyond the scope of optimization and cannot be undone by the decoder. That is, there is no way to make up for bad information in later translation steps.

Another approach is non-deterministic. This provides the decoder with both the original and the reordered source sentence. (Crego and Mariño, 2007) operate within Ngram-based SMT. They make use of syntactic structure to reorder the input into a word lattice. Since the paths are not weighted, the lattice merely narrows down the size of the search space. The decoder is not given reason to trust one path (reordering) over another.

(Zhang et al., 2007) assign weights to the paths of their input word lattice. Instead of hierarchical linguistic structure, they use reordering rules based on POS and syntactic chunks, and train the system with both original and reordered source word order on a restricted data set (<500K words). Their system does not out-perform a standard PSMT system. As they themselves point out, a reason for this might be that their reordering approach is not fully integrated with PSMT. This is one of the main problems addressed in the present work.

(Li et al., 2007) use weighted n-best lists as input for the decoder. They use rules based on a syntactic parse, allowing children of a tree node to swap place. This is excessively restrictive. For example, a common reordering in English-Danish translation has the subject change place with the finite verb. Since the verb is often embedded in a VP containing additional words that should not be moved, such rules cannot be captured by local reordering on tree nodes.

In many cases, the exact same word order that is obtained through a source sentence reordering, is also accessible through a phrase internal reordering. A negative consequence of source order (SO) scoring as done by (Zhang et al., 2007) and (Li et al., 2007) is that they bias against the valuable phrase internal reorderings by only promoting the source sentence reordering. As described in section 4.3, we solve this problem by reordering the input string, but scoring the output string, thus allowing the strengths of PSMT to co-exist with rule-based reordering.

3 Language comparison

The two languages examined in this investigation, English and Danish, are very similar from a structural point of view. A word alignment will most often display an almost one-to-one correlation. In the hand-aligned data, only 39% of the sentences contain reorderings (following the notion of reordering as defined in 4.1). On average, a sentence contains 0.66 reorderings.

One of the main differences between English and Danish word order is that Danish is a verb-second language: the finite verb of a declarative main clause must always be the second constituent. Since this is not the case for English, a reordering rule should move the subject of an English sentence to the right of the finite verb, if the first position is filled by something other than the subject. This is exemplified by (1) (examples are annotated with English gloss and translation), where 'they' should move to the right of 'come' to get the Danish word order as seen in the gloss.

(1) nu kommer de
[now come **they**]
'here ***they*** *come'*

Another difference is that Danish sentence adverbials in a subordinate clause move to the left of the finite verb. This is illustrated in example (2). This example also shows the difficulty for a PSMT system. Since the trigram 'han kan ikke' is frequent in Danish main clauses, and 'han ikke kan' is frequent in subordinate clauses, we need information on subordination to get the correct word order. This information can be obtained from the conjunction 'that'. A trigram PSMT system would not be able to handle the reordering in (2), since 'that' is beyond the scope of 'not'.

(2) han siger at han ikke kan se
[he says that he **not** can see]
'he says that he can ***not*** *see'*

In the main clause, on the other hand, Danish prefers the sentence adverbial to appear to the right of the finite verb. Therefore, if the English adverbial appears to the left of the finite verb in a main clause, it should move right as exemplified by example (3).

(3) hun så aldrig skibet
[she saw **never** the ship]
'she ***never*** *saw the ship'*

Other differences are of a more conventionalized nature. E.g. address numbers are written after the street in Danish (example (4)).

(4) han bor nygade 14
[he lives nygade 14]
'he lives at 14 nygade'

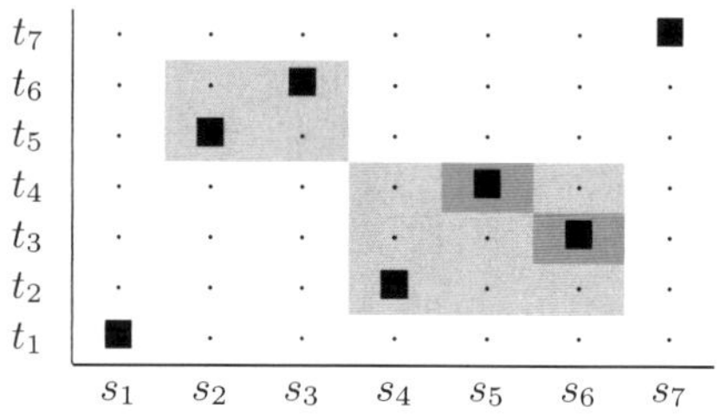

Table 1: Reordering example

4 Reordering rules

4.1 Definition of reordering

In this experiment, reordering is defined as two word sequences exchanging positions. These two sequences are restricted by the following conditions:

- **Parallel consecutive:** They have to make up consecutive sequences of words, and each has to align to a consecutive sequence of words.
- **Maximal:** They have to be the longest possible consecutive sequences changing place.
- **Adjacent:** They have to appear next to each other on both source and target side.

The sequences are not restricted in length, making both short and long distance reordering possible. Furthermore, they need not be phrases in the sense that they appear as an entry in the phrase table.

Table 1 illustrates reordering in a word alignment matrix. The table contains reorderings between the light grey sequences (s_2^3 and s_4^6)[1] and the dark grey sequences (s_5^5 and s_6^6). On the other hand, the sequences s_3^3 and s_4^5 are e.g. not considered reordered, since neither are maximal, and s_4^5 is not consecutive on the target side.

4.2 Rule induction

In section 3, we pointed out that subordination is very important for word order differences between English and Danish. In addition, the sentence position of constituents plays a role. All this information is present in a syntactic sentence parse. A subordinate clause is defined as inside an SBAR con-

[1] Notation: s_x^y means the consecutive source sequence covering words x to y.

Level	LC	LS	RS	RC
WORD	<s> today , || today , || ,	he	was driving	home || home . || home . < /s>
POS	<S> NN , || NN , || ,	PRP	AUX VBG	NN || NN . || NN . < /S>
PS	<S> NP , || NP , || ,	NP	AUX VBG	ADVP || ADVP . || ADVP . < /S>
SUBORD	main	main	main	main

Table 2: Example of experience for learning. Possible contexts separated by ||.

stituent; otherwise it is a main clause. The constituent position can be extracted from the sentence start tag and the following syntactic phrases. POS and word form are also included to allow for more specific/lexicalized rules.

Besides including this information for the candidate reordering sequences (left sequence (LS) and right sequence (RS)), we also include it for the set of possible left (LC) and right (RC) contexts of these. The span of the contexts varies from a single word to all the way to the sentence border. Table 2 contains an example of the information available to the learning algorithm. In the example, LS and RS should change place, since the first position is occupied by something other than the subject in a main clause.

In order to minimize the training data, word and POS sequences are limited to 4 words, and phrase structure (PS) sequences are limited to 3 constituents. In addition, an entry is only used if at least one of these three levels is not too long for both LS and RS, and too long contexts are not included in the set. This does not constrain the possible length of a reordering, since a PS sequence of length 1 can cover an entire sentence.

In order to extract rules from the annotated data, we use a rule-based classifier, Ripper (Cohen, 1996). The motivation for using Ripper is that it allows features to be sets of strings, which fits well with our representation of the context, and it produces easily readable rules that allow better understanding of the decisions being made. In section 6.2, extracted rules are exemplified and analyzed.

The probabilities of the rules are estimated using Maximum Likelihood Estimation based on the information supplied by Ripper on the performance of the individual rules on the training data. These logarithmic probabilities are easily integratable in the log-linear PSMT model as an additional parameter by simple addition.

The rules are extracted from the hand-aligned, Copenhagen Danish-English Dependency Treebank (Buch-Kromann et al., 2007). 5478 sentences from the news paper domain containing 111,805 English words and 100,185 Danish words. The English side is parsed using a state-of-the-art statistical English parser (Charniak, 2000).

4.3 Integrating rule-based reordering in PSMT

The integration of the rule-based reordering in our PSMT system is carried out in two separate stages:

1. Reorder the source sentence to assimilate the word order of the target language.

2. Score the target word order according to the relevant rules.

Stage 1) is done in a non-deterministic fashion by generating a word lattice as input in the spirit of e.g. (Zens et al., 2002; Crego and Mariño, 2007; Zhang et al., 2007). This way, the system has both the original word order, and the reorderings predicted by the rule set. The different paths of the word lattice are merely given as equal suggestions to the decoder. They are in no way individually weighted.

Separating stage 2) from stage 1) is motivated by the fact that reordering can have two distinct origins. They can occur because of stage 1), i.e. the lattice reordering of the original English word order (phrase *external* reordering), and they can occur inside a single phrase (phrase *internal* reordering). We are, however, interested in doing *phrase-independent*, word reordering. We want to promote rule-predicted reorderings, regardless of whether they owe their existence to a syntactic rule or a phrase table entry.

This is accomplished by letting the actual scoring of the reordering focus on the target string. The de-

Source sentence:	today_1 $,_2$ he_3 was_4 late_5	
Rule:	$3\ 4 \rightarrow 4\ 3$	
Hypothesis	Target string	SPTO
H1	idag han var	1 3 4
H2	idag var han	1 4 3

Table 3: Example of SPTO scoring during decoding at source word 4.

coder is informed of where a rule has predicted a reordering, how much it costs to do the reordering, and how much it costs to avoid it. This is then checked for each hypothezised target string by keeping track of what *source position target order* (SPTO) it corresponds to.

The SPTO is a representation of which source position the word in each target position originates from. Putting it differently, the hypotheses contain two parallel strings; a target word string and its SPTO string. In order to access this information, each phrase table entry is annotated with its internal word alignment, which is available as an intermediate product from phrase table creation. If a phrase pair has multiple word alignments, the most frequent is chosen.

Table 3 exemplifies the SPTO scoring. The source sentence is 'today he was late', and a rule has predicted that word 3 and 4 should change place. When the decoder has covered the first four input words, two of the hypothesis target strings might be H1 and H2. At this point, it becomes apparent that H2 contains the desired SPTO (namely '4 3'), and it get assigned the reordering cost. H1 does not contain the rule-suggested SPTO (in stead, the words are in the order '3 4'), and it gets the violation cost. Both these scorings are performed in a phrase-independent manner. The decoder assigns the reordering cost to H2 without knowing whether the reordering is internal (due to a phrase table entry) or external (due to a syntactic rule).

Phrase internal reorderings at other points of the sentence, i.e. points that are not covered by a rule, are not judged by the reordering model. Our rule extraction does not learn every possible reordering between the two languages, but only the most general ones. If no rule has an opinion at a certain point in a sentence, the decoder is free to chose the phrase translation it prefers without reordering cost.

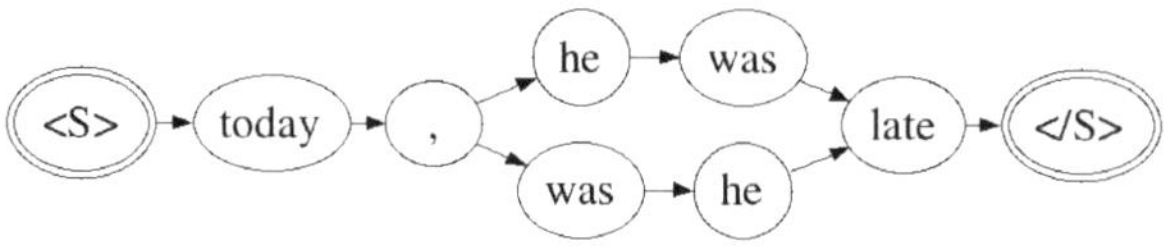

Figure 1: Example word lattice.

Separating the scoring from the source language reordering also has the advantage that the SPTO scoring in essence is compatible with other approaches such as a traditional PSMT system. We will, however, not examine this possibility further in the present paper.

5 The PSMT system

The baseline is the PSMT system used for the 2006 NAACL SMT workshop (Koehn and Monz, 2006) with phrase length 3 and a trigram language model (Stolcke, 2002). The system was trained on the English and Danish part of the Europarl corpus version 3 (Koehn, 2005). Fourth quarter of 2000 was removed in order to use *the common test set* of 11369 sentences (330,082 English words and 309,942 Danish words with one reference) for testing. In addition, fourth quarter of 2001 was removed for development purposes. Of these, 10194 were used for various analysis purposes, thereby keeping the test data perfectly unseen. 500 sentences were taken from the development set for tuning the decoder parameters. This was done using the Downhill Simplex algorithm. In total, 1,137,088 sentences containing 31,376,034 English words and 29,571,518 Danish words were left for training the phrase table and language model.

The decoder used for the baseline system is Pharaoh (Koehn, 2004) with its distance-penalizing reordering model. For the experiments, we use our own decoder which — except for the reordering model — uses the same knowledge sources as Pharaoh, i.e. bidirectional phrase translation model and lexical weighting model, phrase and word penalty, and target language model. Its behavior is comparable to Pharaoh when doing monotone decoding.

The search algorithm of our decoder is similar to the RG graph decoder of (Zens et al., 2002). It ex-

System	Dev	Test	Swap Subset
Baseline	0.262	0.252	0.234
no scoring	0.267	0.256	0.241
SO scoring	0.268	0.258	0.244
SPTO scoring	0.268	0.258	0.245

Table 4: BLEU scores for different scoring methods.

System	BLEU	Avr. Human rating
Baseline	0.234	3.00 (2.56)
no scoring	0.240	3.00 (2.74)
SO scoring	0.239	3.00 (2.62)
SPTO scoring	0.244	2.00 (2.08)

Table 5: Evaluation on the set where SO and SPTO produce different translations. Average human ratings are medians with means in parenthesis, lower scores are better, 1 is the best score.

pects a word lattice as input. Figure 1 shows the word lattice for the example in table 3.

Since the input format defines all possible word orders, a simple monotone search is sufficient. Using a language model of order n, for each hypothezised target string ending in the same n-1-gram, we only have to extend the highest scoring hypothesis. None of the others can possibly outperform this one later on. This is because the maximal context evaluating a phrase extending this hypothesis, is the history (n-1-gram) of the first word of that phrase. The decoder is not able to look any further back at the preceeding string.

6 Evaluation

6.1 Results and discussion

The SPTO reordering approach is evaluated on the 11369 sentences of *the common test set*. Results are listed in table 4 along with results on the development set. We also report on the *swap subset*. These are the 3853 sentences where the approach actually motivated reorderings in the test set, internal or external. The remaining 7516 sentences were not influenced by the SPTO reordering approach.

We report on 1) the baseline PSMT system, 2) a system provided with a rule reordered word lattice but no scoring, 3) the same system but with an SO scoring in the spirit of (Zhang et al., 2007; Li et al., 2007), and finally 4) the same system but with the SPTO scoring.

The SPTO approach gets an increase over the baseline PSMT system of 0.6 % BLEU. The swap subset, however, shows that the extracted rules are somewhat restricted, only resulting in swap in $\frac{1}{3}$ of the sentences. The relevant set, i.e. the set where the present approach actually differs from the baseline, is therefore the swap subset. This way, we concentrate on the actual focus of the paper, namely the syntactically motivated SPTO reordering. Here we achieve an increase in performance of 1.1 % BLEU.

Comparing to the other scoring approaches does not show much improvement. A possible explanation is that the rules do not apply very often, in combination with the fact that the SO and SPTO scoring mechanisms most often behave alike. The difference in SO and SPTO scoring only leads to a difference in translation in 10% of the sentences where reordering is done. This set is interesting, since it provides a focus on the difference between the SO and the SPTO approaches. In table 5, we evaluate on this set.

The BLEU scores on the entire set indicate that SPTO is a superior scoring method. To back this observation, the 100 first sentences are manually evaluated by two native speakers of Danish. (Callison-Burch et al., 2007) show that ranking sentences gives higher inter-annotator agreement than scoring adequacy and fluency. We therefore employ this evaluation method, asking the evaluators to rank sentences from the four systems given the input sentence. Ties are allowed. The annotators had reasonable inter-annotator agreement ($\kappa = 0.523, P(A) = 0.69, P(E) = 0.35$). Table 5 shows the average ratings of the systems. This clearly shows the SPTO scoring to be significantly superior to the other methods ($p < 0.05$).

Most of the cases (55) where SPTO outperforms SO are cases where SPTO knows that a phrase pair contains the desired reordering, but SO does not. Therefore, SO has to use an external reordering which brings poorer translation than the internal reordering, because the words are translated individually rather than by a single phrase (37 cases), or it has to reject the desired reordering (18 cases), which also hurts translation, since it does not get the correct word order.

Decoder choice	SO	SPTO
Phrase internal reordering	401	1538
Phrase external reordering	3846	2849
Reject reordering	1468	1328

Table 6: The choices made based on the SO and SPTO scoring for the 5715 reorderings proposed by the rules for the test data.

No	LC	LS	RS	RC
1	PS: <S> PP ,	PS: NP	POS: FV	
2	PS: SBAR ,	PS: NP	POS: FV	
3	PS: ADVP , ! WORD: however ,	PS: NP	POS: FV	
4		PS: FV	POS: RB	PS: VP SUB: sub
5	PS: <S> NP SUB: main	PS: ADVP	POS: FV	

Table 7: Example rules and their application statistics.

Table 6 shows the effect of SO and SPTO scoring in decoding. Most noticeable is that the SO scoring is strongly biased against phrase internal reorderings; SPTO uses nearly four times as many phrase internal reorderings as SO. In addition, SPTO is a little less likely to reject a rule proposed reordering.

6.2 Rule analysis

The rule induction resulted in a rule set containing 27 rules. Of these, 22 concerned different ways of identifying contexts where a reordering should occur due to the verb second nature of Danish. 4 rules had to do with adverbials in main and in subordinate clauses, and the remaining rule expressed that currency is written after the amount in Danish, while it is the other way around in English. Since the training data however only includes Danish Crowns, the rule was lexicalized to 'DKK'.

Table 7 shows a few of the most frequently used rules. The first three rules deal with the verb second phenomenon. The only difference among these is the left context. Either it is a prepositional phrase, a subordinate clause or an adverbial. These are three ways that the algorithm has learned to identify the verb second phenomenon conditions. Rule 3 is interesting in that it is lexicalized. In the learning data, the Danish correspondent to 'however' is most often not topicalized, and the subject is therefore not forced from the initial position. As a consequence, the rule states that it should only apply, if 'however' is not included in the left context of the reordering.

Rule 4 handles the placement of adverbials in a subordinate clause. Since the right context is subordinate and a verb phrase, the current sequences must also be subordinate. In contrast, the fifth rule deals with adverbials in a main clause, since the left context noun phrase is in a main clause.

A problem with the hand-aligned data used for rule-induction is that it is out of domain compared to the Europarl data used to train the SMT system. The hand-aligned data is news paper texts, and Europarl is transcribed spoken language from the European Parliament. Due to its spoken nature, Europarl contains frequent sentence-initial forms of address. That is, left adjacent elements that are not integrated parts of the sentence as illustrated by example (5).

This is not straightforward, because on the surface these look a lot like topicalized constructions, as in example (6). In topicalized constructions, it is an integrated part of the sentence that is moved to the front in order to affect the flow of discourse information. This difference is crucial for the reordering rules, since 'i' and 'have' should reorder in (6), but not in (5), in order to get Danish word order.

(5) mr president , i have three points .

(6) as president , i have three points .

When translating the development set, it became clear that many constructions like (5) were reordered by a rule. Since these constructions were not present in the hand-aligned data, the learning algorithm did not have the data to learn this difference.

We therefore included a manual, lexicalized rule stating that if the left context contained one of a set of titles (mr, mrs, ms, madam, gentlemen), the reordering should not take place. Since the learning includes word form information, this is a rule that the learning algorithm is able to learn. To a great extent, the rule eliminates the problem.

The above examples also illustrate that local reordering (in this case as local as two neighboring words) can be a problem for PSMT, since even though the reordering is local, the information about whether to reorder or not is not necessarily local.

1	S	based on this viewpoint , **every small port and every ferry port which handles a great deal of tourist traffic** *should* feature on the european list .
	B	baseret på dette synspunkt , **ethvert lille havn og alle færgehavnen som håndterer en stor turist trafik** *skal* stå på den europæiske liste .
	P	baseret på dette synspunkt , *skal* **alle de små havne , og alle færgehavnen som behandler mange af turister trafik** stod på den europæiske liste .
2	S	the rapporteur **generally** *welcomes* the proposals in the commission white paper on this subject but is apprehensive of the possible implications of the reform , which *aims* **principally** to decentralise the implementation of competition rules .
	B	ordføreren **generelt** *bifalder* forslagene i kommissionens hvidbog om dette emne , men er bekymret for de mulige konsekvenser af den reform , som *sigter* **hovedsagelig** at decentralisere gennemførelsen af konkurrencereglerne .
	P	ordføreren *bifalder* **generelt** forslagene i kommissionens hvidbog om dette emne , men er bekymret for de mulige konsekvenser af den reform , som **især** *sigter* mod at decentralisere gennemførelsen af konkurrencereglerne .

Table 8: Examples of reorderings. S is source, B is baseline, and P is the SPTO approach. The elements that have been reordered in the P sentence are marked alike in all sentences. The text in bold has changed place with the text in italics.

6.3 Reordering analysis

In this section, we will show and discuss a few examples of the reorderings made by the SPTO approach. Table 8 contain two translations taken from the test set.

In translation 1), the subject (bold) is correctly moved to the right of the finite verb (italics), which the baseline system fails to do. Moving the finite verb away from the infinite verb 'feature', however, leads to incorrect agreement between these. While the baseline correctly retains the infinite form ('stå'), the language model forces another finite form (the past tense 'stod') in the SPTO reordering approach.

Translation 2) illustrates the handling of adverbials. The first reordering is in a main clause, therefore, the adverbial is moved to the right of the finite verb. The second reordering occurs in a subordinate clause, and the adverbial is moved to the left of the finite verb. Neither of these are handled successfully by the baseline system.

In this case, the reordering leads to better word selection. The English 'aims to' corresponds to the Danish 'sigter mod', which the SPTO approach gets correct. However, the baseline system translates 'to' to its much more common translation 'at', because 'to' is separated from 'aims' by the adverbial 'principally'.

7 Conclusion and Future Plans

We have described a novel approach to word reordering in SMT, which successfully integrates syntactically motivated reordering in phrase-based SMT. This is achieved by reordering the input string, but scoring on the output string. As opposed to previous approaches, this neither biases against phrase internal nor external reorderings. We achieve an absolute improvement in translation quality of 1.1 % BLEU. A result that is supported by manual evaluation, which shows that the SPTO approach is significantly superior to previous approaches.

In the future, we plan to apply this approach to English-Arabic translation. We expect greater gains, due to the higher need for reordering between these less-related languages. We also want to examine the relation between word alignment method and the extracted rules and the relationship between reordering and word selection. Finally, a limitation of the current experiments is that they only allow rule-based external reorderings. Since the SPTO scoring is not tied to a source reordering approach, we want to examine the effect of simply adding it as an additional parameter to the baseline PSMT system. This way, all external reorderings are made possible, but only the rule-supported ones get promoted.

References

Y. Al-Onaizan and K. Papineni. 2006. Distortion models for statistical machine translation. In *Proceedings of 44th ACL.*

M. Buch-Kromann, J. Wedekind, and J. Elming. 2007. The Copenhagen Danish-English Dependency Treebank v. 2.0. http://www.isv.cbs.dk/~mbk/cdt2.0.

C. Callison-Burch, C. Fordyce, P. Koehn, C. Monz, and J. Schroeder. 2007. (Meta-) evaluation of machine translation. In *Proceedings of ACL-2007 Workshop on Statistical Machine Translation.*

E. Charniak. 2000. A maximum-entropy-inspired parser. In *Proceedings of the 1st NAACL.*

W. Cohen. 1996. Learning trees and rules with set-valued features. In *Proceedings of the 14th AAAI.*

M. Collins, P. Koehn, and I. Kucerova. 2005. Clause restructuring for statistical machine translation. In *Proceedings of the 43rd ACL.*

J. M. Crego and J. B. Mariño. 2007. Syntax-enhanced n-gram-based smt. In *Proceedings of the 11th MT Summit.*

N. Habash. 2007. Syntactic preprocessing for statistical machine translation. In *Proceedings of the 11th MT Summit.*

P. Koehn and C. Monz. 2006. Manual and automatic evaluation of machine translation between european languages. In *Proceedings on the WSMT.*

P. Koehn, F. J. Och, and D. Marcu. 2003. Statistical phrase-based translation. In *Proceedings of NAACL.*

P. Koehn. 2004. Pharaoh: a beam search decoder for phrase-based statistical machine translation models. In *Proceedings of AMTA.*

P. Koehn. 2005. Europarl: A parallel corpus for statistical machine translation. In *Proceedings of MT Summit.*

C. Li, M. Li, D. Zhang, M. Li, M. Zhou, and Y. Guan. 2007. A probabilistic approach to syntax-based reordering for statistical machine translation. In *Proceedings of the 45th ACL.*

A. Stolcke. 2002. Srilm – an extensible language modeling toolkit. In *Proceedings of the International Conference on Spoken Language Processing.*

C. Wang, M. Collins, and P. Koehn. 2007. Chinese syntactic reordering for statistical machine translation. In *Proceedings of EMNLP-CoNLL.*

F. Xia and M. McCord. 2004. Improving a statistical mt system with automatically learned rewrite patterns. In *Proceedings of Coling.*

R. Zens, F. J. Och, and H. Ney. 2002. Phrase-based statistical machine translation. In M. Jarke, J. Koehler, and G. Lakemeyer, editors, *KI - 2002: Advances in Artificial Intelligence. 25. Annual German Conference on AI.* Springer Verlag.

Y. Zhang, R. Zens, and H. Ney. 2007. Improved chunk-level reordering for statistical machine translation. In *Proceedings of the IWSLT.*

Experiments in discriminating phrase-based translations on the basis of syntactic coupling features

Vassilina Nikoulina and Marc Dymetman
Xerox Research Centre Europe
Grenoble, France
{nikoulina,dymetman}@xrce.xerox.com

Abstract

We describe experiments on discriminating English to French phrase-based translations through the use of syntactic "coupling" features. Using a robust rule-based dependency parser, we parse both the English source and the French translation candidates from the n-best list returned by our phrase-based system; we compute for each candidate a number of coupling features, that is, values that depend on the amount of alignment between edges in the source and target structures, and discriminatively train the weights of these coupling features. We compare different feature combinations. Although the improvements in terms of automatic measures such as Bleu and Nist are inconclusive, an initial human assessment of the results appears to show certain qualitative improvements.

1 Introduction

1.1 Motivation

When we use the phrase-based SMT system MATRAX (Simard et al., 2005) to translate the sentence *Our declaration of rights is the first of this millenium* from English to French, the result returned by the system is the erroneous translation *Notre déclaration des droits de la première est de ce millénaire*, while somewhere down the n-best list of lesser-scored candidates we find a correct translation: *Notre déclaration des droits est la première de ce millénaire*.

On closer inspection, the difference of scores between the two candidates is the following. In the second (correct) case, the phrase *of rights* was translated into the phrase *des droits*, while in the first (incorrect) case, the phrase *of* was translated into the phrase *de* and the phrase *rights* into the phrase *des droits*. However, while the two bi-phrases *of/de* and *rights/des droits* independently make perfect sense, the sequence *de des droits* in French is not possible, a situation which is easily detected by a standard ngram language model; the language model has then a tendency to try to place the (in fact superfluous) *de* at a further place in the target (just before *la première*), where it is more acceptable to it. The overall consequence is a translation that while formally possible from the viewpoint of a simple language model, is not an adequate representation of the meaning of the source.

Now suppose that we parse both the source and the two candidates with a dependency parser. If we compare the parses of the source and of the correct translation, we find a close (in the current example, very close) isomorphism between dependency edges connecting pairs of aligned words (s_1, s_2) and (t_1, t_2), where s_i is aligned to t_i: the presence of an edge between s_1 and s_2 often implies that of an edge between t_1 and t_2. This is less the case if we compare the parses of the source and of the incorrect translation; in this case, the word *première* is now linked to *droits*, while the word *first* was linked to *millenium*.

While this is of course just one example, it does help to motivate the approach we have taken: we compute different measures of association strength between edges in the source and target dependency trees, and use these measures as features for rerank-

Proceedings of the Second ACL Workshop on Syntax and Structure in Statistical Translation (SSST-2), pages 55–60,
ACL-08: HLT, Columbus, Ohio, USA, June 2008.

ing the n-best candidates of a baseline phrase-based system. The hope is that by doing so, we will increase the adequacy of translations, and possibly to some extent, their fluency (at least their "semantic" fluency, which is influenced by their adequacy, as opposed to their "grammatical" fluency, which would be better addressed by target-specific syntactic features than by coupling syntactic features).

1.2 Related Work

There is a growing body of work on the use of syntax for improving statistical machine translation, from approaches such as (Chiang, 2007) that use "formal syntax", that is syntactic structures for the source and target that are discovered on the basis of a bilingual corpus, but without resort to an externally motivated parser, to approaches such as (Yamada and Knight, 2001) and (Marcu et al., 2006) that use an external parser on the target only, or such as (Quirk et al., 2005) on the source only, or such as (Cowan et al., 2006) that use external parsers both on the source and on the target.

Our approach is in this last category, but is distinguished from all the cited approaches by the fact that it does not try to build a target structure (or string) directly, but rather by using a baseline *phrase-based system* as a generator of candidates, and then selecting between these candidates through a discriminative procedure. Some other researchers have taken a similar line, for example (Hasan et al., 2006), which only uses a parser on the target, and attempts to improve the fluency of the translation produced, and especially (Och et al., 2003) that reports experiments using a large number of syntactic features. In one of the experiments briefly reported, a dependency parser is used both for the source and for the target and a few features are introduced for counting the number of edges that project from the source to the target. This experiment, which as far as we know was not followed up by deeper investigations, is very similar to what we do. However we introduce and compare results for a wider variety of coupling features, taking into account different combinations involving normalization of the counts, symmetrized features between the source and target, labelled dependencies, and also consider several ways for computing the word alignment on the basis of which edge couplings are determined.

2 The approach

2.1 Background

Matrax. The phrase-based SMT system Matrax (Simard et al., 2005), developed at Xerox, was used in the experiments. Matrax is based on a fairly standard log-linear model, but one original aspect of the system is the use of non-contiguous biphrases. Most existing phrase-based models depend on phrases that are sequences of contiguous words on either the source or the target side (e.g. *prendre feu / catch fire*). By contrast, Matrax considers pairs of non-contiguous phrases, such as *ne ... plus / not ... anymore*, where words in the source and target phrases may be separated by gaps, to be filled at translation time by lexical material provided by some other such pairs. One motivation behind this approach is that, basically, the fact that the source expression *ne ... plus* is a good predictor of *not ... anymore* does not depend on the lexical material appearing inside the source expression, an insight which is generally unexploitable by models based on contiguous phrases.[1]

XIP. For parsing, we used the *Xerox Incremental Parser* XIP (Aït-Mokhtar et al., 2002), which is a robust dependency parser developed at the Xerox Research Centre Europe. XIP is fast (around 2000 words per second for English) and is well adapted to a situation, like the one we have here, were we need to parse on the order of a few hundred target candidates on the fly. Also of interest to us is the fact that XIP produces labelled dependencies, a feature that we use in some of our experiments.

2.2 Decoding and Training

Coupling features such as the ones we use require access to the parses of candidate translations, and these parses, at least for a parser such as XIP (and for many similar parsers), can only be obtained once the complete candidate translation is known. This is why it is difficult to introduce them internally in the Matrax stack-based decoder, which would require to provide partial parses for *prefixes* of the target candidates and also associated heuristics to estimate the syntactic structure of completions of these prefixes.

[1]The Hiero system (Chiang, 2007) is a well-known instance of a structure-oriented system that also has a notion of gapped phrases, but contrary to Hiero, Matrax is based on non-hierarchical phrases.

Instead, we resort to a standard reranking approach in which we produce an n-best list of Matrax candidate translations (with n = 100 in our experiments), and then rerank this list with a linear combination of our parse-dependent features. In order to train the feature weights, we use an averaged structured perceptron approach à la Collins, where we try to learn weights such that the first candidate to emerge is equal to the "oracle" candidate, that is, the candidate that is closest to the reference in terms of NIST score.

2.3 Coupling Features

Our general approach to computing coupling features between the dependency structure of the source and that of a candidate translation produced by Matrax is the following: we start by aligning the words between the source and the candidate translation, we parse both sides, and we count (possibly according to a weighting scheme) the number of configurations ("rectangles") that are of the following type: $((s_1, s_{12}, s_2), (t_1, t_{12}, t_2))$, where s_{12} is an edge between s_1 and s_2, t_{12} is an edge between t_1 and t_2, s_1 is aligned with t_1 and s_2 is aligned with t_2. We implemented several variants of this basic scheme.

We start by describing different "generic" coupling functions derived from the basic scheme, assuming that word alignments have been already determined, then we describe the option of taking into account specific dependency labels when counting rectangles, and finally we describe two options for computing the word alignments.

2.3.1 Generic features

The first measure of coupling is based on simple, non-weighted, word alignments. Here we simply consider that a word of the source and a word of the target are aligned or not aligned, without any intermediary degree, and consider that a rectangle exists on the quadruple of words s_1, s_2, t_1, t_2 iff s_i is aligned to t_i, s_1 and s_2 have a dependency link between them (in whatever direction) and similarly for t_1 and t_2. The first feature that we introduce, *Coupling-Count*, is simply the count of all such rectangles between the source and the target.

We note that the value of this feature tends to be correlated with the size of the source and target dependency trees. We therefore introduce some normalized variants of the feature:

- *Coupling-Recall.* We compute the number of source edges for which there exists a projection in the target. More formally, the number of edges between two words s_1, s_2 such that there exist two words t_1, t_2 with s_i aligned to t_i and such that t_1, t_2 have an edge between them. We then divide this number by the total number of edges in the source.

- *Coupling-Precision.* We do the same thing this time starting from the target.

- *Coupling-F-measure.* In the case of perfectly isomorphic dependency trees (a situation that of course rarely occurs because of the linguistic divergences between languages), we would have precision and recall both equal to 1. In order to measure divergence from this ideal case, we introduce a feature that we call *Coupling-F-measure*, which is defined as the harmonic mean of the two previous features.

One deficiency of the previous measures is that they rely a lot on "hard" word alignments, but do not take into account the probability of aligning a source and a target word. We introduce another feature *Coupling-Lex* that exploits lexical translation probabilities: each rectangle found between the source and target trees is weighted according to the product of the translation probabilities associated with (s_1, t_1) and (s_2, t_2).

2.3.2 Label-specific features

The features previously defined do not take into account the labels associated with edges in the dependency trees. However, while rectangles of the form $((s_1, \text{subj}, s_2), (t_1, \text{subj}, t_2))$ may be rather systematic between such languages as English and French, other rectangles may be much less so, due on the one hand to actual linguistic divergences between the two languages, but also, as importantly in practice, to different representational conventions used by different grammar developers for the two languages.[2]

In order to control this problem, we introduce a collection of *Label-Specific-Coupling* features, each for a specific pair of source label and target label.

[2] Although the XIP formalism is shared between grammar developers of French and English, the grammars do sometimes follow slightly different conventions.

The values of a label-specific feature are the number of occurrences for this specific label pair. We use only label pairs that have been observed to be aligned in the training corpus (that is, that participate in observed rectangles). In one version of that approach, we use all such pairs found in the corpus, in another version only the pairs above a certain frequency threshold in the corpus.

2.3.3 Giza-based alignment

In order to compute the features described above, a prerequisite is to be able to determine a word alignment between the source and a candidate translation. Our first approach is to use GIZA++ to create these alignments, by producing for a given source and a given candidate translation n-best alignment lists in both directions and applying standard techniques of symmetrization to produce a bidirectional alignment.

2.3.4 Phrase-based alignment

Another way to find word alignments is to use the information provided by our baseline system. Since Matrax is a phrase-based system, it has access to the bi-phrases (aligned by definition) that are used in order to generate a candidate translation. However note that if we use the bi-phrases directly we are not able to establish the alignments on a word level (since Matrax does not provide any information about word alignments inside the bi-phrases), but only on a phrase level, and we need to adapt the coupling features accordingly.

To overcome this problem, we will transform the dependencies between words into dependencies between phrases. Thus, two phrases c_1, c_2 will have a dependency edge between them if there exists a dependency edge between a word $w_1 \in c_1$ and a word $w_2 \in c_2$. Once this transformation is done both for the source and the target, we get dependency graphs having phrases as nodes. We also know the alignments between these phrases, implicit in the bi-phrases used by Matrax. So, we can consider the phrases as *super-words*, and introduce coupling features of the same type as before, but operating on a higher level (super-words) this time.

3 Experiments

3.1 Description

For all our experiments we use the training, development and test sets provided for the English-French News Commentary corpus in WMT-08. The number of sentences in these sets are respectively 55039, 1057 and 1064, and the average sentence length is 21 words (English) and 24.5 words (French).

We take Matrax as the baseline system. With this system we generate 100-best lists of candidate translations for all source sentences of the test set, we rerank these candidates using our features, and we output the top candidate. We present our results in Table 1, distinguished according to the actual combination of features used in each experiment.

- The *Baseline* entry in the table corresponds to Matrax results on the test set, without the use of any of the coupling features.
- We distinguish two sub-tables, according to whether Giza-based alignments or phrase-based alignments were used.
- The *Generic* keyword corresponds to the coupling features introduced in section 2.3.1, based on rectangle counts, independent of the labels of the edges.
- The *Matrax* keyword corresponds to using Matrax "internal" features as reranking features, along with the coupling features. These Matrax features are pretty standard phrase-based features, apart from some features dealing explicitly with gapped phrases, and are described in detail in (Simard et al., 2005).
- The *Labels* and *Frequent Labels* keywords corresponds to using label-specific features. In the first case (Labels) we extracted all of the aligned label pairs (label pair associated with a coupling rectangle) found in a training set of 1000 source sentences along with their 100-best Matrax translations (this set was chosen to be different from the development set in order to avoid overfitting effects when reranking on the development set); we then obtained 2053 features of this kind. In the second case

	NIST	BLEU	-	+	Diff
Baseline	6.4093	0.2034	0	0	0
Giza-based alignments					
Generic	6.3383	0.2043	15	17	2
Generic, Matrax	*6.3782*	*0.2083*	*4*	*18*	*14*
Labels	6.3483	0.1963	12	18	6
Labels, Generic	6.3514	0.2010	3	18	15
Labels, Generic, Matrax	*6.4016*	*0.2075*	*3*	*20*	*17*
Frequent Labels	6.3815	0.2054	7	11	4
Frequent Labels, Generic	6.3826	0.2044	6	18	12
Frequent Labels, Generic, Matrax	*6.4177*	*0.2100*	*2*	*16*	*14*
Phrase-based alignments					
Generic	6.2869	0.1964	12	14	2
Generic, Matrax	*6.3972*	*0.2031*	*4*	*11*	*7*
Labels	6.3677	0.1995	16	15	-1
Labels, Generic	6.3567	0.1977	8	15	7
Labels, Generic, Matrax	*6.4269*	*0.2049*	*4*	*17*	*13*
Frequent Labels	6.3701	0.1998	3	15	12
Frequent Labels, Generic	6.3846	0.2013	7	16	9
Frequent Labels, Generic, Matrax	*6.4160*	*0.2049*	*4*	*16*	*12*
Giza Generic, Phrase Generic, Giza Labels, Matrax	*6.4351*	*0.2060*	*7*	*22*	*15*

Table 1: Reranking results.

(Frequent Labels), we only kept the most frequently observed among these label pairs, retaining only 137 such features.

- When several keywords appear on a line, we used the union of the corresponding features, and in the last line of the table, we show a combination involving at the same time some features computed on the basis of Giza-based alignments and of phrase-based alignments.

- Along with the NIST and BLEU scores of each combination[3], we also conducted an informal manual assessment of the quality of the results relative to the Matrax baseline. We took a random sample of 100 source sentences from the test set and for each sentence, assessed whether the first candidate produced by reranking was better, worse, or indistinguishable in terms of quality relative to the baseline translation. We report the number of improvements (+) and deteriorations (-) among these 100 samples as well as their difference.

[3]These scores were computed on the basis of only one reference.

3.2 Discussion of the results

While the overall results in terms of Bleu and Nist do not show major improvements relative to the baseline, there are several interesting observations to make. First of all, if we focus on feature combinations in which Matrax features are included (shown in italics in the table), we see that there is a general tendency for the results, both in terms of automatic and human evaluations, to be better than for the same combination without the Matrax features; the explanation seems to be that if we do not use the Matrax features during reranking, but consider the 100 candidates in the n-best list to be equally valuable from the viewpoint of Matrax features, we lose essential information that cannot be recovered simply by appeal to the syntactic coupling features.[4]

If we now concentrate on the lines which do include Matrax features and compare their results with the baseline, we see a trend for these results to be better than the baseline, both in terms of automatic measures as (more strongly) in terms of human eval-

[4]This is not very surprising and probably on the basis of this observation it would be useful in further experiments to introduce as an additional feature the log-linear score given by the Matrax baseline.

uation. Taken individually, perhaps the improvements are not very clear, but *collectively*, a trend does seem to appear in favor of syntactic coupling features generally, although we have not conducted formal statistical tests to validate this impression. A more detailed comparison between individual lines, inside the class of combinations that include Matrax features, appears however difficult to make on the basis of the current experiments.

4 Conclusion and Perspectives

Although there is some consensus that the future of statistical machine translation lies in the use of structural information, it is generally admitted that it is currently difficult to significantly improve over phrase-base systems in this way, at least in terms of automatic evaluation measures. Our results do not contradict that impression, although they are more encouraging in terms of preliminary human assesments than in terms of the automatic measures.

The reranking approach to using syntactic features on top of a phrase-based system is attractive because on the one hand it is easier to implement than a full new syntax-aware decoder, and on the other hand it guarantees at least as good performance as the baseline phrase-based system, if some precautions are taken. On the other hand, its main limitations concern the size of the n-best list of candidates that is realistic in terms of decoding time.[5] At least two approaches seem promising in order to alleviate this problem: (1) find a way to capitalize on the factorization of translation candidates in the internal lattice used by the phrase-based decoder, in order to produce factorized parses that would permit comparison between more candidates than can be seen through a final n-best list; (2) allow the reranker to perform local transformations of the n-best candidates, in the spirit of (Langlais et al., 2007), in order to be able to explore a larger space of promising candidates than is provided by the static list.

Another interesting direction would be to learn the feature weights by reranking towards another type of oracle than the one we used, which is defined as the closest candidate in the list in terms of NIST score relative to the reference; instead it might be worthwhile to use as an oracle the candidate in the list which receives the best human assessment in terms of fluency and adequacy, giving a better chance to the syntactic features to show their worth; but this would probably also require that these systems be mostly evaluated in terms of human assessment, a trend which is more and more noticeable in the SMT community.

[5] It should be noted however that we could increase this size from 100 to 1000 without incurring too much penalty, given the speed of the XIP parser we use.

References

Salah Aït-Mokhtar, Jean-Pierre Chanod, and Claude Roux. 2002. Robustness beyond shallowness: incremental deep parsing. *Natural Language Engineering*, 8(3):121–144.

David Chiang. 2007. Hierarchical phrase-based translation. *Computational Linguistics*, 33(2):201–228.

Brooke Cowan, Ivona Kucerova, and Michael Collins. 2006. A discriminative model for tree-to-tree translation. In *Proceedings EMNLP*.

Saša Hasan, Oliver Bender, and Hermann Ney. 2006. Reranking translation hypotheses using structural properties. In *Proceedings of the EACL Workshop on Learning Structured Information in Natural Language Applications*.

Philippe Langlais, Alexandre Patry, and Fabrizio Gotti. 2007. A greedy decoder for phrase-based statistical machine translation. In *Proceedings of the 11th International Conference on Theoretical and Methodological Issues in Machine Translation*, pages 104–113, Skvde, Sweden, Sept.

D. Marcu, W. Wang, A. Echihabi, and K. Knight. 2006. SPMT: Statistical Machine Translation with Syntactified Target Language Phrases. In *Proceedings EMNLP*, pages 44–52.

Franz Josef Och, Daniel Gildea, Sanjeev Khudanpur, Anoop Sarkar, Kenji Yamada, Alex Fraser, Shankar Kumar, Libin Shen, David Smith, Katherine Eng, Viren Jain, Zhen Jin, and Dragomir Radev. 2003. Syntax for statistical machine translation: Final report of john hopkins 2003 summer workshop. Technical report, John Hopkins University.

Chris Quirk, Arul Menezes, and Colin Cherry. 2005. Dependency treelet translation: Syntactically informed phrasal SMT. In *ACL05*.

Michel Simard, Nicola Cancedda, Bruno Cavestro, Marc Dymetman, Éric Gaussier, Cyril Goutte, Kenji Yamada, Philippe Langlais, and Arne Mauser. 2005. Translating with non-contiguous phrases. In *HLT/EMNLP*.

Kenji Yamada and Kevin Knight. 2001. A syntax-based statistical translation model. In *Proceedings ACL*, pages 531–538.

Multiple Reorderings in Phrase-based Machine Translation

Niyu Ge, Abe Ittycheriah
IBM T.J.Watson Research
1101 Kitchawan Rd.
Yorktown Heights, NY 10598
(niyuge, abei)@us.ibm.com

Kishore Papineni
Yahoo! Research
45 West 18th St.
New York, NY 10011
kpapi@yahoo-inc.com

Abstract

This paper presents a method to integrate multiple reordering strategies in phrase-based statistical machine translation. Recently there has been much research effort in reordering problems in machine translation. State-of-the-art decoders incorporate sophisticated local reordering strategies, but there is little research on a unified approach to incorporate various kinds of reordering methods. We present a phrase-based decoder which easily allows multiple reordering schemes. We show how to use this framework to perform distance-based reordering and HIERO-style (Chiang 2005) hierarchical reordering. We also present two novel syntax-based reordering methods, one built on part-of-speech tags and the other based on parse trees. We will give experimental results using these relatively easy to implement methods on standard tests.

1 Introduction and Previous Work

Given an input source sentence and guided by a translation model, language model, distortion model, etc., a machine translation decoder searches for a target sentence that is the best translation of the source. There are usually two aspects of the search. One tries to find target words for a given source segment. The other searches for the order in which the source segments are to be translated. A source *segment* here means a contiguous part of the source sentence. The former is largely controlled by language models and translation models and the latter by language models and distortion models. It is, in most cases, the latter, the search for the correct word order (which source segment to be translated next) that results in a large combinatorial search space. State-of-the-art decoders use dynamic programming based beam-search with local reordering (Och 1999, Tillmann 2000). Although local reordering to some degree is implicit in phrase-based decoding, the kind of reordering is very limited. The simplest distance-based reordering, from the current source position *i*, tries to defer the translation of the next *n* words ($1 \leq n \leq N$, N the maximum number of words to be delayed). N is bounded by the computational requirements.

Recent work on reordering has been on trying to find "smart" ways to decide word order, using syntactic features such as POS tags (Lee and Ge 2005) , parse trees (Zhang et.al, 2007, Wang et.al. 2007, Collins et.al. 2005, Yamada and Knight 2001) to name just a few, and synchronized CFG (Wu 1997, Chiang 2005), again to name just a few. These efforts have shown promising improvements in translation quality. However, to use these features during decoding requires either a separate decoder to be written or some ad-hoc mechanisms to be invented to incorporate them into an existing decoder, or in some cases (Wang et. al. 2007) the input source is pre-ordered to be decoded monotonically.

(Kanthak et. al. 2005) described a framework in which different reordering methods are represented as search constraints to a finite state automata. It is able to compute distance-based and ITG-style reordering automata. We differ from that approach in a couple of ways. One is that in (Kanthak et. al. 2005), an on-demand

Proceedings of the Second ACL Workshop on Syntax and Structure in Statistical Translation (SSST-2), pages 61–68,
ACL-08: HLT, Columbus, Ohio, USA, June 2008.

reordering graph is pre-computed which is then taken as a input for monotonic decoding. We compute the reordering as the sentence is being decoded. The second is that it is not clear how to generate the permutation graphs under, say HIERO-type hierarchical constraints, or other syntax-inspired reorderings such as those based on part-of-speech patterns. Our approach differs in that we allow greater flexibility in capturing a wider range of reordering strategies.

We will first give an overview of the framework (§2). We then describe how to implement four reordering methods in a single decoder in §3. §4 presents some Chinese-English results on the NIST MT test sets. It also shows results on web log and broadcast news data.

2 Reordering in Decoding

2.1 Hypothesis

The process of MT decoding can be thought of as a process of hypothesizing target translations. Given an input source sentence of length L, the decoding is done segment by segment. A *segment* is simply an n-word source chunk, where $1 \leq n \leq L$. Decoding finishes when all source chunks are translated (some source words that have no target translations can be thought of as being translated into a special token NULL). The decoder at this point outputs its best hypothesis.

2.2 Hypothesis with reorderings

In order to facilitate various search strategies, a separation of duty is called for. The decoder is composed of two major modules, a reordering module and a production module. The reordering module decides which source segment to be translated next. The production module produces the actual translations for a given segment. Although most of the start-of-the-art decoders have these two modules, they are nevertheless tightly coupled. Here they are separated. This separation does not compromise the search space of the decoder. Hypotheses that are explored in the traditional way are still explored in this framework. This separation is essential if one were to design a decoder that incorporates phrase-based, syntax-based, and other types of decoding in a unified and disciplined way. In the decoder, each hypothesis carries with it a sequence of source segments to be decoded at the current time step. After the production module translates these segments and after beam pruning is applied to all the hypotheses produced at this time step, the hypotheses go back to the reordering module which determines the next source segments to be translated. This process continues until all source words are translated.

One can think of the reordering module as a black box whose sole responsibility is to determine the next sequence of source segments to be translated. Given this separation, the reordering module can be implemented in whichever way and the changes in it do not require changes to any other modules in the decoder. There can be a suite of such modules, each exploring different features and implementing different search schemes. A reordering module that implement basic distance-based reordering will take two parameters, the number of source words to be skipped and the window size that determines when the skipped words must be translated. A reordering module that is based on HIERO rules will take the library of HIERO rules and select the subset that fire on a given input sentence. The module will use this subset of rules to determine the source translation order. A parse-inspired reordering module will take an input parse tree and based on either a trained model or hand-written rules decide the next source sequence to be translated. As long as all the reordering modules are written to a common interface, they can be separately written and maintained.

Figure 1 shows an example of how three reordering modules can be incorporated into a single decoder. The input source is $S_1 \ldots S_n$.

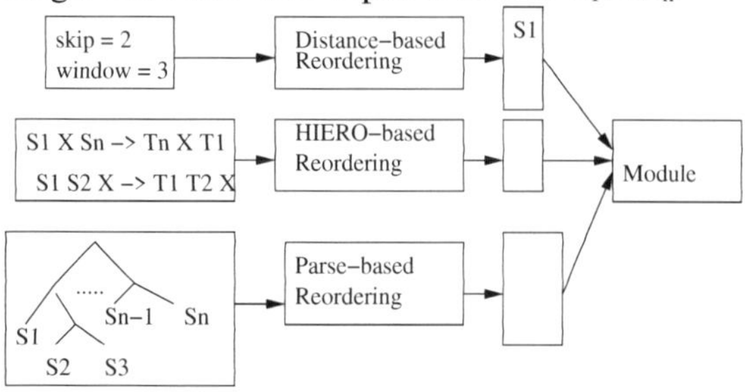

Figure 1. Reordering module example

Each reordering module has its own resources and parameters which are shown on the left side. Each reordering module produces a vector of next source positions. The production module takes these positions and produces translations for them.

3 Reordering Modules

In this section, we describe four reordering modules implementing different reordering strategies. The framework is not limited to these four methods. We present these four to demonstrate the ability of the framework to incorporate a wide variety of reordering methods.

3.1 Distance-based Skip Reordering

This is the type of reordering first presented by (Brown et.al. 1993) and was briefly alluded to in the above *Introduction* section. This method is controlled by 2 parameters:

Skip = number of words whose translations are to be delayed. Let us call these words *skipped* words.

WindowWidth (ww) = maximum number of words allowed to be translated before translating the skipped words.

This reordering module outputs all the possible next source words to be translated according to these two parameters. For illustration purposes, let us use a bit vector ***B*** to represent which source words have been translated. Thus those that have been translated have value 1 in the bit vector, and those un-translated have 0. As an example, let skip = 2 and ww = 3, and an input sentence of length = 10. Initially, all 10 entries of B are 0. At the first time step, only the following are possible next positions:

a) 1 0 0 0 0 0 0 0 0 0 : translate 1st word
b) 0 1 0 0 0 0 0 0 0 0 : skip 1st word
c) 0 0 1 0 0 0 0 0 0 0 : skip 1st and 2nd words

At the next time step, if we want to continue the path of c), we have these choices:
1) we can leave the first 2 words open and continue until we reach 3 words (because ww=3)

c1) 0 0 1 1 0 0 0 0 0 0
c2) 0 0 1 1 1 0 0 0 0 0

2) or we can go back and translate either of the first 2 skipped words:

c3) 1 0 1 0 0 0 0 0 0 0
c4) 0 1 1 0 0 0 0 0 0 0

It is clear that the search space easily blows up with large skip and window-width values. Therefore, a beam pruning step is performed after partial hypotheses are produced at every time step.

3.2 HIERO Hierarchical Reordering

In this section we show an example of how the Hiero decoding method (Chiang 2005) can be implemented as a reordering module in this framework. This is not meant to show that our MT decoder is a synchronous CFG parser. This is a conceptual demonstration of how the Hiero rules can be used in a reordering module to decide the source translation order and thus used in a traditional phrase-based decoder. This module uses the Hiero rules to determine the next source segment to be translated. The example is Chinese-English translation. Consider the following Chinese sentence (word position and English gloss are shown in parentheses):

澳大利亚(1.Australia) 是(2. is) 与(3. with) 北韩(4. North Korea) 有(5. have) 邦交(6. diplomatic relation) 的(7. NULL) 少数(8. few) 国家(9. country) 之一(10. one of)

Suppose we have two following Hiero rules:

澳大利亚 X → Australia X (1)
是 X 之一 → is one of X (2)

The left-hand-side of Hiero rules are source phrases and the right-hand-side is their English translation and the Xs are the non-terminals whose extent is determined by the source input against which the rules are tested for matching. A rule fires if its left-hand-side matches certain segments of the input.

Given the above Chinese input and the two Hiero rules, the Hiero decoder as described in (Chiang 2005) will produce a partial hypothesis "*Australia is one of*" by firing the two rules during parsing (see Chiang 2005 for decoding details). We will show how to decode in the Hiero paradigm using the framework.

The reordering module first decides a source segment based on rule (1). Rule (1) generates a sequence of source segments in term of source ranges: <[1,1],[2,10]>. This means the source segment spanning range [1,1] (word 1, *澳大利亚 /Australia*) is to be translated first, and then the remaining segment spanning range [2,10] is to be translated next. This is exactly what rule (1) dictates where *澳大利亚* corresponds to source [1,1] in the reordering module's output and the *X* is [2,10]. The range [1,1], after being given to the production module, results in the production of a partial hypothesis where the target "*Australia*" is produced. The task now is to translate the next source range [2,10]. At this point, the reordering module generates another source segment according to rule (2) where the left-hand-side "*是 X 之一*" is matched against the input and three corresponding source ranges are found which are *[2,2] (是/is)*, *[4,9] (X)*, and *[10,10] (之一/one of)*. According to rule (2), this source sequence is to be translated in the order of *[2,2] (is)*, *[10,10] (one of)*, and then *[4,9] (X)*. Therefore the output of the reordering module at this stage is *<[2,2],[10,10],[4,9]>*. This would then go on to be translated and results in a partial hypothesis to "*Australia is one of*". Thus "*Australia is one of*" is a partial production which covers source segments [1,1] [2,2] and [10,10] in that order. Note that the source segments decoded so far are not contiguous and this is the effect of long-range reordering imposed by rule (2). The next stage is <[4,9]> which is what the *X* in rule (2) corresponds to. From here onwards, other rules will fire and the decoding sequence these rules dictate will be realized by the reordering module in the form of source ranges. This process can also be viewed hierarchically in Figure 2.

In Figure 2 the ranges (the bracketed numbers) are source segments and the leaves are English productions. Initially we have the whole input sentence as one range [1,10]. According to rule (1), this initial range is refined to be *<[1,1],[2,10]>*, the 2nd level in Figure 2. The [2,10] is further refined by rule (2) to generate the 3rd level ranges *<[2,2],[10,10],[4,9]>* and the process goes on. Ranges that cannot be further refined go into the production module which

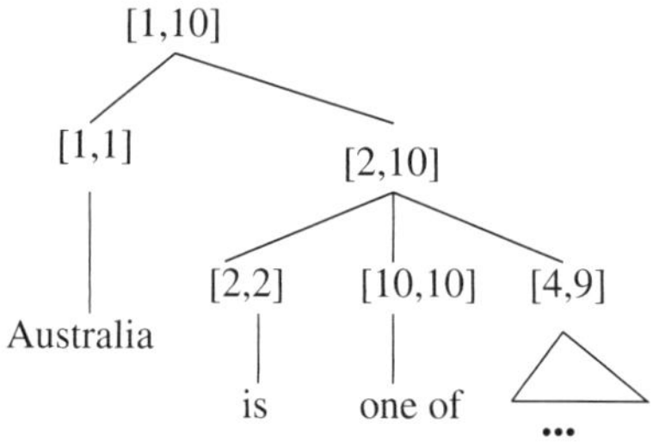

Figure 2. Hiero-style decoding

generates partial hypotheses which are the leaves in the figure. In other words, the partial hypotheses are generated by traversing the tree in Figure 2 in a left-to-right depth-first fashion.

3.3 Generalized Part-Of-Speech-based Reordering

The aim of a generalized part-of-speech-based reordering method is to tackle the problem of long-range word movement. Chinese is a pre-modification language in which the modifiers precede the head. The following is an example with English gloss in parentheses. The prepositional modifier "*on the table*" follows the head "*the book*" in English (3.3b), but precedes it in Chinese (3.3a). When the modifiers are long, word-based local reordering is inadequate to handle the movement.

3.3a. 桌(*table*) 上(*on*) 的(NULL) 书(*book*)
3.3b. the book on the table

There have been several approaches to the problem some of which are mentioned in §1. Compared to these methods, this approach is lightweight in that it requires only part-of-speech (POS) tagging on the source side. The idea is to capture general long-distance distortion phenomena by extracting reordering patterns using a mixture of words and part-of-speech tags on the source side. The reordering patterns are extracted for every contiguously aligned source segment in the following form:

$$source\ sequence \rightarrow target\ sequence$$

Both the *source sequence* and the *target sequence* are expressed using a combination of source words and POS tags. The patterns are 'generalized' not only because POS tags are used but also because variables or place-holders are allowed. Given a pair of source and target training sentences, their word alignments and POS tags on the source, we look for any contiguously aligned source segment and extract word reordering patterns around it. Figure 3 shows an example.

Shown in Figure 3 are a pair of Chinese and English sentence, the Chinese POS tags and the word alignment indicated by the lines. When multiple English words are aligned to a single Chinese word, they are grouped by a rectangle for easy viewing. Here we have a contiguously aligned source segment from position 3 to 8. Using the range notation, we say that source range [3,8] is aligned to target range [6, 14]. Let X denote the source segment [3,8]. The source verb phrase (at positions 9 and 10) occur after X whereas the corresponding target verb phrase (target words 2,3, and 4) occur before the translation of X (which is target [6,14]). We thus extract the following pattern:

$$对 X\ V\ N \rightarrow V\ N\ 对 X \qquad (1)$$

where the left-hand side '*对 X V N*' is the source word sequence and the right-hand side '*V N 对X*' is the target word sequence. The *X* in the pattern is meant to represent a variable, to be matched by a sequence of source words in the test data when this pattern fires during decoding. Note that the pattern is a mixture of words and POS tags. Specifically, the word identity of the preposition 对 (position 2) is retained whereas the content words (the verb and the noun) are substituted by their POS tags. This is because in general, for the reordering purpose the POS tags are good class representations for content words whereas different prepositions may have different word order patterns so that mapping them all to a single POS *P* masks the difference. Examples of patterns are shown in Table 1.

In Chinese-English translation, the majority of the reorderings occur around verb modifiers (prepositions) and noun modifiers (usually around the Chinese part-of-speech DEG as in position 6). Therefore we choose to extract only these 2 kinds of patterns that involve a preposition and/or a DEG. In the example above, there are only 2 such patterns:

$$对 X\ V\ N \rightarrow V\ N\ 对 X \qquad (1)$$

$$X_1\ DEG\ X_2 \rightarrow X_2\ DEG\ X_1 \qquad (2)$$

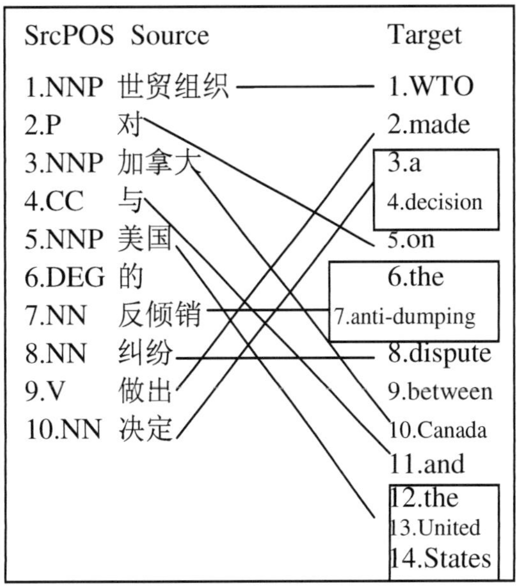

Figure 3. Chinese/English Alignment Example

	Source Seq.	Target Seq.	Count	P(tseq |sseq)
1	X DEG NN	X DEG NN	861	0.198
2	X DEG NN	X NN DEG	1322	0.305
3	X DEG NN	NN DEG X	2070	0.477
4	X DEG NN	NN X DEG	10	0.002
5	X DEG NN	DEG NN X	52	0.012
6	X DEG NN	DEG X NN	22	0.005
7	由 X VV	由 X VV	15	0.118
8	由 X VV	VV 由 X	112	0.882
9	因为X VV	VV 因为 X	2	0.041
10	因为X VV	因为X VV	47	0.959

Table 1. Pattern examples

In the table, we see that when the preposition is 由 (rows 7 and 8, translation: *by*), then the swapping is more likely (0.882 in row 8). When the preposition is 因为 (rows 9 and 10 translation: *because*), then the target most often stays the same order as the source (prob 0.959, last row).

3.4 Parse-based Lexicalized Reordering

Part-of-speech reordering patterns as described in §3.3 are crude approximation to the structure of the source sentence. For example, in the source pattern 'X DEG NN', the variable X can match a source segment of arbitrary length which is followed by 'DEG NN'. Although it does capture very long range movement as a result of

X matching a long segment, it often searches unnecessarily for those segments that are implausible matches to X. The goal of the pattern 'X DEG NN' is to capture the pre-modification phenomenon in Chinese where X is to match a modifier. Parse trees are good at capturing these structures. A parse tree is shown in Figure 4a using notation from Chinese Treebank CHTB5 (nodes with same label are numbered for easy reference).

The node CP has 2 children, first of which is an IP and second is the word whose POS is DEG. This tree denotes a big NP (top node NP1) whose head is the rightmost NP (NP2). The IP under the CP is the modifier. Given this tree, we can easily tell the span of the modifier IP.

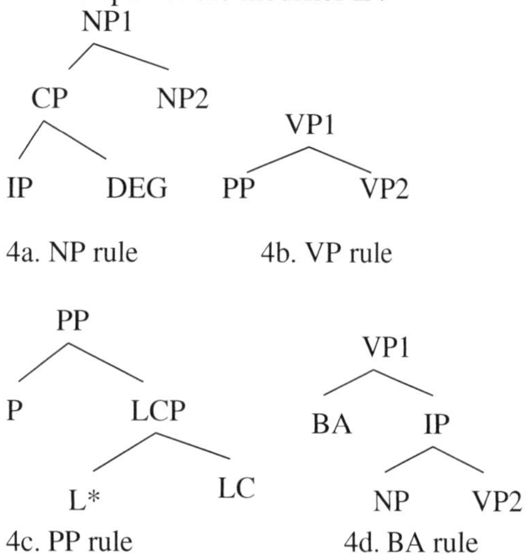

Figure 4. Source parse trees to be reordered

Parse trees represent the whole structure of the entire sentence. Not every structure is of interest to the reordering problem. In a way similar to that used in part-of-speech-pattern extraction (§3.3), we restrict our attention to four kinds of structures, the first of which is NP involving a DEG (as in Figure 4a.) The other three are in Figure 4b, 4c, and 4d. In Figure 4c, the label L* means any node, sometimes it is a CP, sometimes an IP, and so on.

Figure 4b captures the pre-modification in case of a VP where PP modifies VP2 in Chinese and needs to be swapped when translating into English. Figure 4c is the case where there are both pre-position (P) and post-position (LC) in the Chinese. In English, there are only pre-positions and therefore something must be done to the post-position LC. Figure 4d is the construction in Chinese that turns an SVO word order into SOV and here we want VP2 to precede its object NP.

The reordering rules are written using the leaves in the parse tree, in other words, the lexical items. In the rules below, we use the bracketed label [L] to mean the leaves it covers, so [NP] means the leaves under NP. The reordering rules for the 4 structures are:
NP (Figure 4a): [NP2] [DEG] [IP]
VP (Figure 4b): [VP2] [PP]
PP (Figure 4c): [P] [LC] [L*]
BA (Figure 4d): [VP2] [NP]

Figure 5 is an example of rule 4a.

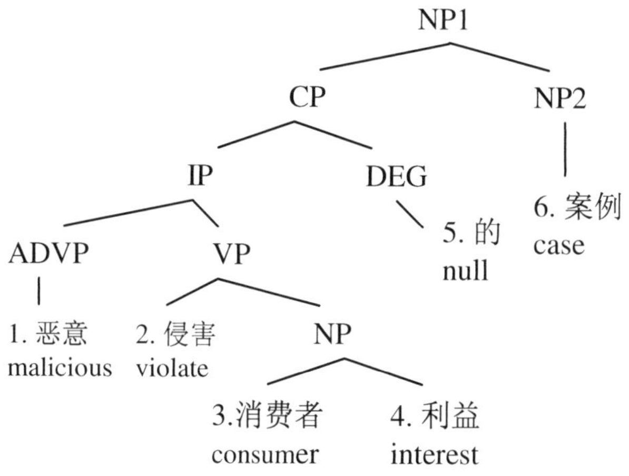

Figure 5. Lexical example of NP rule

Chinese words and their English gloss are written at the leaves. The correct English translation is "*cases of malicious violation of consumer interests*". The DEG in the tree signals that the preceding IP is the modifier of the head NP2. Given this tree, the reordering rule is [NP2] [DEG] [IP] (see 4a) which will be written in the form

source sequence → *target sequence*

which is realized as the following (the indices are for easy reference and are not in the actual rule)
1.恶意 2.侵害病 3.消费者 4.利益 5.的 6.案例 →
6.案例 5.的 1.恶意 2.侵害病 3.消费者 4.利益

The first three of these structures are explored in (Wang et.al. 2007). The crucial difference is that in (Wang et.al. 2007), the reordering rules for these structures are used as a hard decision to pre-order the source. Here the rules are used to extract reorder patterns which are used as an integral part of the decoder. The reordering module not only proposes the next source segment according to the reordering patterns but also proposes monotone choices. This is because first, the parser is errorful. In this work, we use the Stanford Parser (Levy and Manning 2003). On the last 929 sentences of CHTB5, the parser achieves 81% label F-measure on true CHTB5 word segmentation and drops to 65% on system segmentation using the Stanford CRF Segmenter (Tseng et.al. 2005). The second reason to let the decoder choose between reordering and monotone is other modules such as phrase tables and target LM can have an influence on the order choice too, especially when both reorder and monotone are acceptable as in the following example:

CH: 我(my/mine/I/me) 的(DEG/null) 书(book)
English1: my book (monotone)
English2: the book of mine (reorder)

Since the Chinese has a DEG, our reordering rule will prefer to swap but monotone is often correct. In cases like these we let the other models, such as TM and LM, to also have a say in deciding the outcome. The reordering module will present both choices to be produced.

4 Experiment Results

We run our experiments on NIST Chinese-English MT03 and MT04 and also on weblog (WL) and broadcast news (BN) data. The WL and BN test sets are held-out data from LDC-released parallel training data. WL data is from LDC2006E34 and BN is from LDC2006E10. The metric reported is cased *BLEUn4* 4-gram BLEU (Papineni et.al. 2001).

We train HMM alignments in both direction to get source-to-target and target-to-source probabilities. We have a smoothed 5-gram English LM built on the English Gigaword corpus and the English side of the Chinese-English parallel corpora distributed by LDC from year 2000 to 2005.

For distance-based skip reordering (§3.1) we experimented with four sets of skip and WindowWidth values.

For part-of-speech reordering patterns, we use the 3259 hand alignments contained in LDC2006E93. We build a MaxEnt Chinese POS tagger and tagged the Chinese side of this data. The tagger achieves 92% F-measure on the 10% heldout data of CHTB5. We then extracted reordering patterns according to the procedure described in §3.3. A total of 788 source patterns were extracted. It is a small pattern set because of our specific extraction criteria described in §3.3. At decoding time, an average of 15-20 patterns fire on a single sentence. We use the unigram probabilities of the rules as shown in Table 1 to score the rules.

For parse-based lexical reordering rules, we run the Stanford parser on the test set and extract the lexicalized patterns. The number of patterns of each test set is shown in Table 2. The reordered rules are assigned a value of 0.9 and the monotones are assigned a value of 0.1.

Test Set	# Sentences	# Lex.Patterns
MT03	919	4,824
MT04	1,788	13,639
WL (LDC2006E34)	550	3,261
BN (LDC2006E10)	2,069	12,492

Table 2. Test data statistics

The results on the NIST MT test sets MT03 and MT04 utilizing 4 references are in shown in Table 3. The results of the weblog and broadcast news data are shown in Table 4 where there is 1 reference for each set. The confidence intervals in these experiments are between ±0.12 and ±0.16. This means the variations in rows 1-5 of Table 3 are not statistically significant. The part-of-speech based reordering shows marginal improvement. We see significant improvement in using parse-based reordering rules.

	Cased-BLEU**r4**n4	MT03	MT04
1	Skip0 (monotone)	0.2817	0.3023
2	Skip = 1; WW=2	0.2854	0.3024
3	Skip = 2; WW = 3	0.2878	0.3061
4	Skip = 3; WW = 4	0.2903	0.3081
5	Skip = 4; WW = 5	0.2833	0.3090
6	Generalized POS	0.3066	0.3182
7	Parse-based Lex	0.3231	0.3250

Table 3. NIST MT03 and MT04 Results

Cased-BLEUr1n4	Weblog	Broadcast News
Skip0 (monotone)	0.0656	0.0858
Generalized POS	0.0694	0.0878
Parse-based Lex	0.0862	0.1135

Table 4. Weblog and BN results

5. Conclusions

We have presented a decoding framework that greatly facilitates the incorporation of various reordering strategies that are necessary to put the words in the right order during translation. This modularized framework abstracts away the reordering phase from the rest of the decoder components. This not only makes the decoder easier to maintain but also allows rapid experimentation of a variety of reordering methods. Instead of using one reordering module, multiple reordering modules are used to come up with a list of next possible source segment choices. So far we have not seen any significant improvement using combination of reordering modules. This warrants further research since intuitively the knowledge-rich modules and the distance-based methods ought to complement each other. The POS and parse-based methods are very targeted and work quite well when the source structure is correctly understood, but cannot correct itself when errors occur in the tagging or the parsing process. The distance-based methods pay no attention to structure and is thus immune from source processing errors.

Although we present the POS-based and parse-based reordering modules in the context of Chinese to English translation, they can be used for other languages as well. For example, in Arabic to English translation, we extract patterns that capture the VSO word order of Arabic (English is SVO) and also the adjectival post-modification of noun.

The framework greatly reduces the amount of work needed to experiment with drastically different ways of reordering. All these can now be done in one single decoder.

Acknowledgements

This work was partially supported by the Department of the Interior, National Business Center under contract No. NBCH2030001 and Defense Advanced Research Projects Agency under contract No. HR0011-06-2-0001. The views and findings contained in this material are those of the authors and do not necessarily reflect the position or policy of the U.S. government and no official endorsement should be inferred.

References

P.F.Brown, S.A.Della Pietra, V.J.Della Pietra, and R.L.Mercer. *The Mathematics of Statistical Machine Translation.* Computation Linguistics, 19(2).

D. Chiang 2005 *A hierarchical phrase-based model for statistical machine translation.* 2005 ACL.

Y.Lee and N.Ge 2006 *Local reordering in statistical machine translation.* Workshop of TCStar 2006

R. Levy and C. Manning. 2003. *Is it harder to parse Chinese, or the Chinese Treebank?* ACL 2003

S. Kanthak, D. Vilar, E. Matusov, R. Zens, and H. Ney. *Novel Reordering Approaches in Phrase-Based Statistical Machine Translation.* In ACL Workshop on Building and Using Parallel Texts 2005

F.Och, P. Koehn, and D. Marcu. 2003. *Statistical phrase-based translation.* HLT-NAACL 2003

F.Och, C.Tillmann, H.Ney 1999 *Improved alignment models for statistical machine ranslation*, EMNLP

F. Och. 2003. *Minimum error rate training in statistical machine translation.* ACL2003

K.Papineni, S.Roukos, T.Ward, W.Zhu 2001. *A method for automatic evaluation for MT,* ACL 2001

C.Tillmann, H. Ney 2000 *Word reordering and DP-based search in SMT*, COLING 2000

H. Tseng, P. Chang, G. Andrew, D. Jurafsky and C. Manning. *A Conditional Random Field Word Segmenter.* In Fourth SIGHAN Workshop 2005.

Dekai Wu. 1997 *Stochastic inversion transduction grammars and bilingual parsing of parallel corpora.* Computational Linguistics, Vol. 23, pp. 377-404

Kenji Yamada and Kevin Knight 2001 *A syntax-based statistical translation model.* ACL 2001

D.Zhang, M. Li, C. Li, and M. Zhou. *Phrase Reordering Model Integrating Syntactic Knowledge for SMT.* Proceedings of EMNLP 2007

C. Wang, M.Collins, and P.Koehn. Chinese Syntactic *Reordering for Statistical Machine Translation.* Proceedings of EMNLP 2007

Improving Word Alignment Using Syntactic Dependencies

Yanjun Ma[1] **Sylwia Ozdowska**[1] **Yanli Sun**[2] **Andy Way**[1]
[1] School of Computing, Dublin City University, Dublin, Ireland
{yma,sozdowska,away}@computing.dcu.ie
[2] School of Applied Language and Intercultural Studies,
Dublin City University, Dublin, Ireland
yanli.sun2@mail.dcu.ie

Abstract

We introduce a word alignment framework that facilitates the incorporation of syntax encoded in bilingual dependency tree pairs. Our model consists of two sub-models: an anchor word alignment model which aims to find a set of high-precision anchor links and a syntax-enhanced word alignment model which focuses on aligning the remaining words relying on dependency information invoked by the acquired anchor links. We show that our syntax-enhanced word alignment approach leads to a 10.32% and 5.57% relative decrease in alignment error rate compared to a generative word alignment model and a *syntax-proof* discriminative word alignment model respectively. Furthermore, our approach is evaluated extrinsically using a phrase-based statistical machine translation system. The results show that SMT systems based on our word alignment approach tend to generate shorter outputs. Without length penalty, using our word alignments yields statistically significant improvement in Chinese–English machine translation in comparison with the baseline word alignment.

1 Introduction

Automatic word alignment can be defined as the problem of determining translational correspondences at word level given a parallel corpus of aligned sentences. Bilingual word alignment is a fundamental component of most approaches to statistical machine translation (SMT). Dominant approaches to word alignment can be classified into two main schools: generative and discriminative word alignment models.

Generative word alignment models, initially developed at IBM (Brown et al., 1993), and then augmented by an HMM-based model (Vogel et al., 1996), have provided powerful modeling capability for word alignment. However, it is very difficult to incorporate new features into these models. Discriminative word alignment models, based on discriminative training of a set of features (Liu et al., 2005; Moore, 2005), on the other hand, are more flexible to incorporate new features, and feature selection is essential to the performance of the system.

Syntactic annotation of bilingual corpora, which can be obtained more efficiently and accurately with the advances in monolingual language processing, is a potential information source for word alignment tasks. For example, Part-of-Speech (POS) tags of source and target words can be used to tackle the data sparseness problem in discriminative word alignment (Liu et al., 2005; Blunsom and Cohn, 2006). Shallow parsing has also been used to provide relevant information for alignment (Ren et al., 2007; Sun et al., 2000). Deeper syntax, e.g. phrase or dependency structures, has been shown useful in generative models (Wang and Zhou, 2004; Lopez and Resnik, 2005), heuristic-based models (Ayan et al., 2004; Ozdowska, 2004) and even for syntactically motivated models such as ITG (Wu, 1997; Cherry and Lin, 2006).

In this paper, we introduce an approach to improve word alignment by incorporating syntactic dependencies. Our approach is motivated by the fact that words tend to be dependent on each other. If

Proceedings of the Second ACL Workshop on Syntax and Structure in Statistical Translation (SSST-2), pages 69–77,
ACL-08: HLT, Columbus, Ohio, USA, June 2008.

we can first obtain a set of reliable anchor links, we could take advantage of the syntactic dependencies relating unaligned words to aligned anchor words to expand the alignment. Figure 1 gives an illustrating example. Note that the link $(2,4)$ can be easily identified, but the link involving the fourth Chinese word (a function word denoting 'time') $(4,4)$ is hard. In such cases, we can make use of the dependency relationship ('tclause') between c_2 and c_4 to help the alignment process. Given such an observation, our model is composed of two related alignment models. The first one is an anchor alignment model which is used to find a set of anchor links; the other one is a syntax-enhanced alignment model aiming to process the words left unaligned after anchoring.

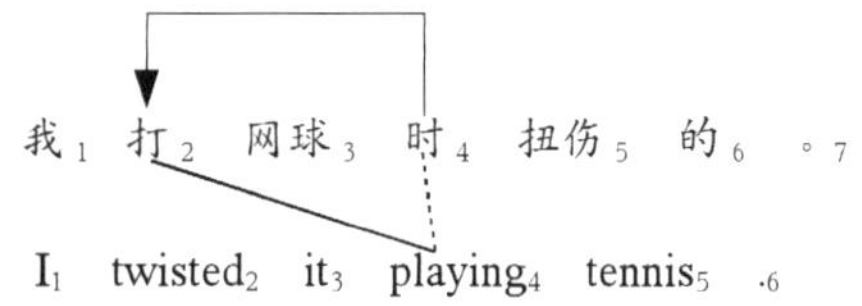

Figure 1: How syntactic dependencies can help word alignment: an example

The remainder of this paper is organized as follows. In Section 2, we introduce our syntax-enhanced discriminative word alignment approach. The feature functions used are described in Section 3. Experimental setting and results are presented in Section 4 and 5 respectively. In Section 6, we compare our approach with other related word alignment approaches. Section 7 concludes the paper and gives avenues for future work.

2 Word Alignment Model

2.1 Notation

While in this paper we focus on Chinese–English, the method proposed is applicable to any language pair. The notation will assume Chinese–English word alignment and Chinese–English MT. Here we adopt a notation similar to (Brown et al., 1993). Given a Chinese sentence c_1^J consisting of J words $\{c_1, ..., c_J\}$ and an English sentence e_1^I consisting of I words $e_1, ..., e_I$, we define the alignment A between c_1^J and e_1^I as a subset of the Cartesian product of the word positions:

$$A \subseteq \{(j,i) : j = 1, ..., J; i = 1, ..., I\}$$

Our alignment representation is restricted so that each source word can only be aligned to one target word. The alignment A consists of associations $j \rightarrow i = a_j$ from a source position j to a target position $i = a_j$. The 'null' alignment $a_j = 0$ with the 'empty' word e_0 is used to account for source words that are not aligned to any target word.

We use A_Δ to denote a subset of A. The indices of the K source words involved in A_Δ are represented as Δ_1^K and the corresponding target indices for Δ_k are represented as a_{Δ_k}. The unaligned source words are represented as $\bar{\Delta}$.

2.2 General Model

Given a source sentence c_1^J and target sentence e_1^I, we seek to find the optimum alignment $\hat{A}$ such that:

$$\hat{A} = \underset{A}{\text{argmax}} P(A|c_1^J, e_1^I) \quad (1)$$

We use a model (2) that directly models the linkage between source and target words similarly to (Ittycheriah and Roukos, 2005). We decompose this model into an anchor alignment model (3) and a syntax-enhanced model (4) by distinguishing the anchor alignment from the non-anchor alignment.

$$\begin{aligned} p(A|c_1^J, e_1^I) &= \prod_{j=0}^{J} p(a_j|c_1^J, e_1^I, a_1^{j-1}) & (2) \\ &= \frac{1}{Z} \cdot p_\epsilon(A_\Delta|c_1^J, e_1^I) \cdot & (3) \\ &\quad \prod_{j \in \bar{\Delta}} p(a_j|c_1^J, e_1^I, a_1^{j-1}, A_\Delta) & (4) \end{aligned}$$

2.3 Anchor Alignment Model

The anchor alignment model $p_\epsilon(A_\Delta)$ aims to find a set of high precision links. Various approaches can be used for this purpose. In this paper we adopted the following two approaches.

2.3.1 Heuristics-based Approach

The problem of word alignment is regarded as a process of word linkage disambiguation, i.e. choosing the correct links between words from all competing hypothesis (Melamed, 2000; Deng and Gao, 2007).

We constrain the link probabilities in such a way that:

$$\forall i' \in \{1, ..., I\}, i' \neq i : \frac{p((j,i))}{p((j,i'))} > \epsilon_1 \quad (5)$$

$$\forall j' \in \{1, ..., J\}, j' \neq j : \frac{p((j,i))}{p((j',i))} > \epsilon_2 \quad (6)$$

Condition (5) implies that for the source word c_j, the link with the target word e_i is more probable (with reliability threshold ϵ_1) than the link with any other target word. Condition (6) guarantees that for the target word e_i, c_j is the only most probable (with threshold ϵ_2) source word to be linked to.

2.3.2 Intersected Generative Word Alignment Models

We can use the asymmetric IBM models for bidirectional word alignment and get the intersection.

2.4 Syntax-Enhanced Word Alignment Model

The syntax-enhanced model is used to model the alignment of the words left unaligned after anchoring. We directly model the linkage between source and target words using a discriminative word alignment framework where various features can be incorporated. Given a source word c_j and the target sentence e_1^I, we search for the alignment a_j such that:

$$\hat{a_j} = \underset{a_j}{\text{argmax}}\{p_{\lambda_1^M}(a_j|c_1^J, e_1^I, a_1^{j-1}, A_\Delta)\} \quad (7)$$

$$= \underset{a_j}{\text{argmax}}\{\textstyle\sum_{m=1}^{M} \lambda_m h_m(c_1^J, e_1^I, a_1^j, A_\Delta, T_c, T_e)\}$$

In this decision rule, we assume that a set of highly reliable anchor alignments A_Δ has been obtained, and T_c (resp. T_e) is used to denote the dependency structure for source (resp. target) language. In such a framework, various machine learning techniques can be used for parameter estimation.

3 Feature Function for Syntax-Enhanced Model

The various features used in our syntax-enhanced model can be classified into three groups: statistics-based features, syntactic features and relative distortion features.

3.1 Statistics-based Features

3.1.1 IBM model 1 score

IBM model 1 is a position-independent word alignment model which is often used to bootstrap parameters for more complex models. Model 1 models the conditional distribution and uses a uniform distribution for the dependencies between source word positions and target word positions.

$$Pr(c_1^J, a_1^J|e_1^I) = \frac{p(J|I)}{(I+1)^J} \prod_{j=1}^{J} p(c_j|e_{a_j}) \quad (8)$$

3.1.2 Log-likelihood ratio

The log-likelihood ratio statistic has been found to be accurate for modeling the associations between rare events (Dunning, 1993). It has also been successfully used to measure the associations between word pairs (Melamed, 2000; Moore, 2005). Given the following contingency table:

	c_j	$\neg c_j$
e_i	a	b
$\neg e_i$	c	d

the log-likelihood ratio can be defined as:

$$G^2(c_j, e_i) = -2log\frac{B(a|a+b, p_1)B(c|c+d, p_2)}{B(a|a+b, p)B(c|c+d, p)}$$

where $B(k|n,p) = \binom{n}{k}p^k(1-p)^{n-k}$ are binomial probabilities. The probability parameters can be obtained using maximum likelihood estimates:

$$p_1 = \frac{a}{a+b}, p_2 = \frac{c}{c+d} \quad (9)$$

$$p = \frac{a+c}{a+b+c+d} \quad (10)$$

3.1.3 POS translation probability

The POS tags can provide effective information for addressing the data sparseness problem using the lexical features (Liu et al., 2005; Blunsom and Cohn, 2006). The POS translation probability can be easily obtained using maximum likelihood estimation from an annotated corpus:

$$Pr(T_c|T_e) = \frac{COL(T_c, T_e)}{COF(T_e)} \quad (11)$$

where T_c is a Chinese word's POS tag and T_e is an English word's POS tag. $COL(T_c, T_e)$ is the count of T_c and T_e being linked to each other in the corpus, and $COF(T_e)$ is the frequency of T_e in the corpus.

3.2 Syntactic Features

The dependency relation R_e (resp. R_c) between two English (resp. Chinese) words e_i and $e_{i'}$ (resp. c_j and $c_{j'}$) in the dependency tree of the English sentence e_1^I (resp. Chinese sentence c_1^J) can be represented as a triple $<e_i, R_e, e_{i'}>$(resp. $<c_j, R_c, e_{j'}>$). Given c_1^J, e_1^I and their syntactic dependency trees $T_{c_1^J}$, $T_{e_1^I}$, if e_i is aligned to c_j and $e_{i'}$ aligned to $c_{j'}$, according to the dependency correspondence assumption (Hwa et al., 2002), there exists a triple $<c_j, R_c, c_{j'}>$.

While we are not aiming to justify the feasibility of the dependency correspondence assumption by proving to what extent $R_e = R_c$ under the condition described above, we do believe that c_j and $c_{j'}$ are likely to be dependent on each other. Given the anchor alignment A_Δ, a candidate link (j, i) and the dependency trees, we can design four classes of feature functions.

3.2.1 Agreement features

The agreement features can be further classified into dependency agreement features and dependency label agreement features. Given a candidate link (j, i) and the anchor alignment A_Δ, the dependency agreement (DA) feature function is defined as follows:

$$h_{DA-1} = \begin{cases} 1 & \text{if } \exists <c_j, R_c, c_{j'}>, <e_i, R_e, e_{i'}> \\ & \text{and } (j', i') \in A_\Delta, \\ 0 & \text{otherwise.} \end{cases} \quad (12)$$

By changing the dependency direction between the words c_j and $c_{j'}$, we can derive another dependency agreement feature:

$$h_{DA-2} = \begin{cases} 1 & \text{if } \exists <c_{j'}, R_c, c_j>, <e_{i'}, R_e, e_i> \\ & \text{and } (j', i') \in A_\Delta, \\ 0 & \text{otherwise.} \end{cases} \quad (13)$$

We can define the dependency label agreement feature[1] as follows:

$$h_{DLA-1} = \begin{cases} 1 & \text{if } \exists <c_j, R_c, c_{j'}>, <e_i, R_e, e_{i'}> \\ & \text{and } (j', i') \in A_\Delta, R_c = R_e, \\ 0 & \text{otherwise.} \end{cases} \quad (14)$$

Similarly we can obtain h_{DLA-2} by changing the dependency direction.

3.2.2 Source word dependency features

Given a candidate link (j, i) and anchor alignment A_Δ, source language dependency features are used to capture the dependency label between a source word c_j and a source anchor word $c_k \in \Delta$. For example, a feature function relating to dependency type 'PRD' can be defined as:

$$h_{src-1-PRD} = \begin{cases} 1 & \text{if } \exists <c_j, R_c, c_{j'}> \\ & \text{and } R_c = \text{'PRD'}, \\ 0 & \text{otherwise.} \end{cases} \quad (15)$$

By changing the direction we can obtain $h_{src-2-PRD}$.

3.2.3 Target word dependency features

Target word dependency features can be defined in a similar way as source word dependency features.

3.2.4 Target anchor feature

The target anchor feature defines whether the target word e_i is an anchor word.

$$h_{src-1-PRD} = \begin{cases} 1 & \text{if } i \in a_\Delta, \\ 0 & \text{otherwise.} \end{cases} \quad (16)$$

3.3 Relative distortion feature

We can design features encoding the relative distortion information which can be used to evaluate a candidate link by computing its relative position change with respect to the anchor alignment. The relative position change of a candidate link $l = (j, i)$ is formally defined as follows:

[1]Note that we used the same dependency parser for source and target language parsing.

$$D(l) = min(|d_L|, |d_R|) \quad (17)$$

$$d_L = (j - j_L) - (i - i_L) \quad (18)$$

$$d_R = (j - j_R) - (i - i_R) \quad (19)$$

where (i_L, j_L) is the leftmost anchor link of l, (i_R, j_R) is the rightmost anchor link of l. The less the relative position changes, the more likely the candidate link is. With a set of anchor alignments, we can obtain the distribution of the relative position changes from an annotated corpus using maximum likelihood estimation. In our experiments, we used the following four probabilities: $p(D = 0)$, $p(D = 1, 2)$, $p(D = 3, 4)$ and $p(D > 4)$.

4 Experimental Setting

4.1 Data

The experiments were carried out using the Chinese–English datasets provided within the IWSLT 2007 evaluation campaign (Fordyce, 2007), extracted from the Basic Travel Expression Corpus (BTEC) (Takezawa et al., 2002). This multilingual speech corpus contains sentences similar to those that are usually found in phrase-books for tourists going abroad.

We tagged all the sentences in the training and devset3 using a maximum entropy-based POS tagger–MXPOST (Ratnaparkhi, 1996), trained on the Penn English and Chinese Treebanks. Both Chinese and English sentences are parsed using the Malt dependency parser (Nivre et al., 2007), which achieved 84% and 88% labelled attachment scores for Chinese and English respectively.

4.1.1 Word Alignment

We manually annotated word alignments on devset3. Since manual word alignment is an ambiguous task, we also explicitly allow for ambiguous alignments, i.e. the links are marked as sure (*S*) or possible (*P*) (Och and Ney, 2003). IWSLT devset3 consists of 502 sentence pairs after cleaning. We used the first 300 sentence pairs for training, the following 50 sentence pairs as validation set and the last 152 sentence pairs for testing.

4.1.2 Machine Translation

Training was performed using the default training set (39,952 sentence pairs), to which we added the set devset1 (506 sentence pairs).[2] We used devset2 (506 sentence pairs, 16 references) to tune various parameters in the MT system and IWSLT 2007 test set (489 sentence pairs, 6 references) for testing.

4.2 Alignment Training and Search

In our experiments, we treated anchor alignment and syntax-enhanced alignment as separate processes in a pipeline. The anchor alignments are kept fixed so that the parameters in the syntax-enhanced model can be optimized.[3] We used the support vector machine (SVM) toolkit–SVM_light[4] to optimize the parameters in (7). Our model is constrained in such a way that each source word can only be aligned to one target word. Therefore, in training, we transform each possible link involving the words left unaligned after anchoring into an event. In testing, the source words are consumed in sequence and the target words serve as states. The SVM dual variable was used to measure the reliability of each candidate link and the alignment link for each word is made independently, which makes the alignment search much easier. A threshold t was set as the minimal reliability score for each link. t is optimized according to alignment error rate (21) on the validation set.

4.3 Baselines

4.3.1 Word Alignment

We used the GIZA++ implementation of IBM word alignment model 4 (Brown et al., 1993; Och and Ney, 2003) for word alignment, and the heuristics described in (Och and Ney, 2003) to derive the intersection and refined alignment.

4.3.2 Machine Translation

We use a standard log-linear phrase-based SMT (PB-SMT) model as a baseline: GIZA++ implementation of IBM word alignment model 4,[5] the refine-

[2]More specifically, we chose the first English reference from the 16 references and the Chinese sentence to construct new sentence pairs.

[3]Note our anchor alignment does not achieve 100% precision. Since we performed precision-oriented alignment for the anchor alignment model, the errors in anchor alignment will not bring much noise into the syntax-enhanced model.

[4]http://svmlight.joachims.org/

[5]More specifically, we performed 5 iterations of Model 1, 5 iterations of HMM, 3 iterations of Model 3, and 3 iterations of Model 4.

ment and phrase-extraction heuristics described in (Koehn et al., 2003), minimum-error-rate training (Och, 2003), a trigram language model with Kneser-Ney smoothing trained with SRILM (Stolcke, 2002) on the English side of the training data, and Moses (Koehn et al., 2007) to decode.

4.4 Evaluation

We evaluate the intrinsic quality of predicted alignment A with precision, recall and alignment error rate (AER). Slightly differently from (Och and Ney, 2003), we use possible alignments in computing recall.

$$recall = \frac{|A \cap P|}{|P|}, precision = \frac{|A \cap P|}{|A|} \quad (20)$$

$$AER(S, P; A) = 1 - \frac{|A \cap S| + |A \cap P|}{|A| + |S|} \quad (21)$$

We also extrinsically measure the word alignment quality via a Chinese–English translation task. The translation output is measured using BLEU (Papineni et al., 2002).

5 Experimental Results

5.1 Word Alignment

We performed word alignment bidirectionally using our approach to obtain the union and compared our results with two strong baselines based on generative word alignment models. The results are shown in Table 1. We can see that both the syntax-enhanced model based on HMM intersection anchors (Syntax-HMM) and on IBM model 4 anchors (Syntax-Model 4) are better than the pure generative word alignment models. Our approach is superior in precision with a disadvantage in recall. The best result achieved 10.32% relative decrease in AER compared to the baseline when we use IBM model 4 intersection to obtain the set of anchor alignments.

model	precision	recall	f-score	AER
HMM refined	0.8043	0.7592	0.7811	0.2059
Syntax-HMM	0.8744	0.7304	0.7959	0.1845
Model 4 refined	0.7941	0.7987	0.7964	0.1929
Syntax-Model 4	0.8566	0.7685	0.8102	**0.1730**

Table 1: Comparing syntax-enhanced approach with generative word alignment

5.1.1 The Influence of Anchor Alignment Quality

As we can see in Table 2, our precision-oriented approach to acquire anchor alignments was accomplished quite well. All four different anchor alignment models achieved high precision. However, the recall differs dramatically, with model 4 achieving the highest recall and the heuristics-based approach receiving the lowest. To investigate the influence of the anchor alignment model, we first obtained the intersection of the words left unaligned after anchoring using each of the anchor alignment models. We evaluate the alignment of these words against the gold-standard alignments involving these words. The influence of anchor alignment on the performance of the syntax-enhanced model can be seen in Table 3. The performance of the syntax-enhanced model is closely related to that of the anchor alignment method. As can be seen from Table 2 and 3, HMM anchoring achieves the best precision and so does the syntax-enhanced alignment; IBM model 4 achieves the best recall and so does the syntax-enhanced alignment. Finally, the best alignment performances are obtained with IBM model 4 anchoring, with the difference in recall between HMM and IBM model 4 anchoring being more significant than the difference in precision.

anchor model	precision	recall	f-measure	AER
Heuristics	0.9774	0.4047	0.5724	0.3947
Model 1	0.9509	0.5011	0.6563	0.3157
HMM	0.9802	0.5327	0.6903	0.2809
Model 4	0.9777	0.5677	0.7179	0.2533

Table 2: Performance of anchor alignment

anchor model	precision	recall	f-score	AER
Heuristics	0.4505	0.3270	0.3790	0.6210
Model 1	0.5538	0.3894	0.4573	0.5427
HMM	0.5932	0.3611	0.4489	0.5511
Model 4	0.5660	0.4216	0.4832	0.5168

Table 3: Influence of anchor alignment in syntax-enhanced model

5.1.2 The Influence of Syntactic Dependencies on Word Alignment

The influence of incorporating syntactic dependencies into the word alignment process is shown in Table 4. Syntax plays a positive role in all different anchor alignment configurations. The influence grows proportionally to the strength of the anchor alignment model. With the Model 4 intersection used as the set of anchor alignments, adding syntactic dependency features into the syntax-enhanced alignment model yields a 5.57% relative decrease in AER.

model	precision	recall	f-score	AER
Heuristics				
no syntax	0.8362	0.6751	0.7470	0.2302
w. syntax	0.8376	0.6894	0.7563	0.2240
Model 1				
no syntax	0.8759	0.6902	0.7720	0.2045
w. syntax	0.8542	0.7160	0.7790	0.2011
HMM				
no syntax	0.8655	0.7168	0.7841	0.1952
w. syntax	0.8744	0.7304	0.7959	0.1845
Model 4				
no syntax	0.8697	0.7340	0.7961	0.1832
w. syntax	0.8566	0.7685	0.8102	**0.1730**

Table 4: Influence of syntactic dependencies on word alignment

5.1.3 Contribution of Different Feature Classes

We interpret the contribution of each feature in terms of feature weights in SVM model training. The weights for the most discriminative features in each feature class in Chinese–English word alignment (using HMM intersection as anchor alignment) are shown in Table 5. As we can see, all statistics-based features are informative. Two target dependency features are informative: 'PRD' denoting 'predicative' dependency, and 'AMOD' denoting 'adjective/adverb modifier' dependency.

	weight
Model 1 Score	0.1416
POS	0.0540
Log-likelihood Ratio	0.0856
relative distortion	0.0606
DA-1	0.0227
DLA-2	0.0927
tgt-1-PRD	0.0961
tgt-2-AMOD	0.0621

Table 5: Weights of some informative features

5.2 Machine Translation

Research has shown that an increase in AER does not necessarily imply an improvement in translation quality (Liang et al., 2006) and vice-versa (Vilar et al., 2006). Hereafter, we used a Chinese–English MT task to extrinsically evaluate the quality of our word alignment.

Table 6 shows the influence of our word alignment approach on MT quality.[6] On development set, we achieved statistically significant improvement using both our syntax-enhanced models—Syntax-HMM ($p<0.002$) and Syntax-Model 4 ($p<0.008$). On the test set, we observed that the MT output based on our alignment model tends to be shorter than the reference translations and the BLEU score is considerably penalized. If we ignore the length penalty ('BP' in Table 6) in significance testing, the improvement on test set is also statistically significant: $p<0.04$ for both Syntax-HMM and Syntax-Model 4. However, an indepth manual analysis needs to be carried out in order to determine the exact nature of the shorter sentences derived.

	dev. set	test set
Baseline	0.5412	0.3510 (BP=0.96)
Syntax-HMM	0.6015	0.3409 (BP=0.86)
Syntax-Model 4	0.5834	0.3585 (BP=0.91)

Table 6: The Influence of Word Alignment on MT

6 Comparison with Previous Work

Our syntax-enhanced model is a discriminative word alignment model. Certain generative word alignment models (e.g. HMM or IBM 4) also take the first-order dependencies into account. However, long distance dependencies between words are hard to incorporate into these models because of the explosive number of parameters. On the other hand, like existing discriminative models, our approach uses a set of informative features based on co-occurrence statistics, e.g. log-likelihood ratio and DICE score. The advantage of our approach is the mechanism by which syntactic features may be incorporated.

[6] Note that the only difference between our MT system and the baseline PB-SMT system is the word alignment component.

Some previous research also tried to make use of syntax in word alignment. (Wang and Zhou, 2004) investigated the benefit of monolingual parsing for alignment. They learned a generalized word association measure (crosslingual word similarities) based on monolingual dependency structures and improved alignment performances over IBM model 2 and certain heuristic-based models. (Cherry and Lin, 2006) used dependency structures as soft constraints to improve word alignment in an ITG framework. Compared to these models, our approach directly takes advantage of dependency relations as they are transformed into feature functions incorporated into a discriminative word alignment framework.

7 Conclusion and Future Work

In this paper, we proposed a model that can facilitate the incorporation of syntax into word alignment and measured the combination of a set of syntactic features. Experimental results have shown that syntax is useful in word alignment and especially effective in improving the recall. We have also observed that in our word alignment framework, the two submodels are closely related and the quality of the anchor alignment model plays an important role in the system performance.

The promising results will lead us to improve our model in the following aspects. First, the two submodels in our approach are two separate processes performed in pipeline. We plan to jointly optimize the two models in one go. Second, some of our experiments used complex IBM models, e.g. IBM Model 4, to obtain anchor alignment. We plan to boostrap the alignment using simple heuristics without relying on complex IBM models. Third, the alignment searching process assumed the alignment link for each word is made independently. A feasible markovian assumption will be tested for searching. Fourth, a comparison with traditional discriminative word alignment models is also necessary to justify the merits of our approach. Finally, we also plan to adapt our approach to larger data sets and more language pairs.

Acknowledgments

This work is supported by Science Foundation Ireland (grant number OS/IN/1732). Prof. Rebecca Hwa from University of Pittsburgh and Dr. Yang Liu from the Institute of Computing Technology, Chinese Academy of Sciences, are kindly acknowledged for providing us with their word alignment guidelines. We would also like to thank the anonymous reviewers for their insightful comments.

References

Necip Fazil Ayan, Bonnie Dorr, and Nizar Habash. 2004. Multi-align: Combining linguistic and statistical techniques to improve alignments for adaptable mt. In *Proceedings of the 6th Conference of the AMTA (AMTA-2004)*, pages 17–26, Washington DC.

Phil Blunsom and Trevor Cohn. 2006. Discriminative word alignment with conditional random fields. In *Proceedings of the 21st International Conference on Computational Linguistics and 44th Annual Meeting of the Association for Computational Linguistics*, pages 65–72, Sydney, Australia.

Peter F. Brown, Stephen A. Della Pietra, Vincent J. Della Pietra, and Robert L. Mercer. 1993. The mathematics of statistical machine translation: Parameter estimation. *Computational Linguistics*, 19(2):263–311.

Colin Cherry and Dekang Lin. 2006. Soft syntactic constraints for word alignment through discriminative training. In *Proceedings of the 21st International Conference on Computational Linguistics and 44th Annual Meeting of the Association for Computational Linguistics*, pages 105–112, Sydney, Australia.

Yonggang Deng and Yuqing Gao. 2007. Guiding statistical word alignment models with prior knowledge. In *Proceedings of the 45th Annual Meeting of the Association of Computational Linguistics*, pages 1–8, Prague, Czech Republic.

Ted Dunning. 1993. Accurate methods for the statistics of surprise and coincidence. *Computational Linguistics*, 19(1):61–74.

Cameron Shaw Fordyce. 2007. Overview of the IWSLT 2007 Evaluation Campaign. In *Proceedings of the International Workshop on Spoken Language Translation*, pages 1–12, Trento, Italy.

Rebecca Hwa, Philip Resnik, Amy Weinberg, and Okan Kolak. 2002. Evaluating translational correspondence using annotation projection. In *Proceedings of the 40th Annual Meeting of the Association for Computational Linguistics*, pages 392–399, Philadelphia, PA.

Abraham Ittycheriah and Salim Roukos. 2005. A maximum entropy word aligner for Arabic-English machine translation. In *Proceedings of Human Language*

Technology Conference and Conference on Empirical Methods in Natural Language Processing, pages 89–96, Vancouver, British Columbia, Canada.

Philipp Koehn, Franz Och, and Daniel Marcu. 2003. Statistical phrase-based translation. In *Proceedings of Human Language Technology Conference and Conference on Empirical Methods in Natural Language Processing*, pages 48–54, Edmonton, Canada.

Philipp Koehn, Hieu Hoang, Alexandra Birch, Chris Callison-Burch, Marcello Federico, Nicola Bertoldi, Brooke Cowan, Wade Shen, Christine Moran, Richard Zens, Chris Dyer, Ondrej Bojar, Alexandra Constantin, and Evan Herbst. 2007. Moses: Open source toolkit for statistical machine translation. In *Proceedings of the 45th Annual Meeting of the Association for Computational Linguistics Companion Volume Proceedings of the Demo and Poster Sessions*, pages 177–180, Prague, Czech Republic.

Percy Liang, Ben Taskar, and Dan Klein. 2006. Alignment by agreement. In *Proceedings of Human Language Technology Conference and Conference on Empirical Methods in Natural Language Processing*, pages 104–111, New York, NY.

Yang Liu, Qun Liu, and Shouxun Lin. 2005. Log-linear models for word alignment. In *Proceedings of the 43rd Annual Meeting of the Association for Computational Linguistics*, pages 459–466, Ann Arbor, MI.

Adam Lopez and Philip Resnik. 2005. Improved HMM alignment models for languages with scarce resources. In *Proceedings of the ACL Workshop on Building and Using Parallel Texts*, pages 83–86, Ann Arbor, Michigan, June.

I. Dan Melamed. 2000. Models of translational equivalence among words. *Computational Linguistics*, 26(2):221–249.

Robert C. Moore. 2005. A discriminative framework for bilingual word alignment. In *Proceedings of Human Language Technology Conference and Conference on Empirical Methods in Natural Language Processing*, pages 81–88, Vancouver, British Columbia, Canada.

Joakim Nivre, Johan Hall, Jens Nilsson, Atanas Chanev, Gülsen Eryigit, Sandra Kübler, Svetoslav Marinov, and Ervin Marsi. 2007. MaltParser: A language-independent system for data-driven dependency parsing. *Natural Language Engineering*, 13(2):95–135.

Franz Och and Hermann Ney. 2003. A systematic comparison of various statistical alignment models. *Computational Linguistics*, 29(1):19–51.

Franz Och. 2003. Minimum error rate training in statistical machine translation. In *Proceedings of the 41st Annual Meeting of the Association for Computational Linguistics*, pages 160–167, Sapporo, Japan.

Sylwia Ozdowska. 2004. Identifying correspondences between words: an approach based on a bilingual syntactic analysis of French/English parallel corpora. In *Proceedings of the COLING'04 Workshop on Multilingual Linguistic Resources*, pages 49–56, Geneva, Switzerland.

Kishore Papineni, Salim Roukos, Todd Ward, and Wei-Jing Zhu. 2002. BLEU: a method for automatic evaluation of machine translation. In *Proceedings of the 40th Annual Meeting of the Association for Computational Linguistics*, pages 311–318, Philadelphia, PA.

Adwait Ratnaparkhi. 1996. A maximum entropy model for part-of-speech tagging. In Eric Brill and Kenneth Church, editors, *Proceedings of the Conference on Empirical Methods in Natural Language Processing*, pages 133–142, Somerset, NJ.

Dengjun Ren, Hua Wu, and Haifeng Wang. 2007. Improving statistical word alignment with various clues. In *Machine Translation Summit XI*, pages 391–397, Copenhagen, Denmark.

Andrea Stolcke. 2002. SRILM - An extensible language modeling toolkit. In *Proceedings of the International Conference on Spoken Language Processing*, pages 901–904, Denver, CO.

Le Sun, Youbing Jin, Lin Du, and Yufang Sun. 2000. Word alignment of English-Chinese bilingual corpus based on chunks. In *Proceedings of the 2000 Joint SIGDAT conference on Empirical Methods in Natural Language Processing and very large corpora*, pages 110–116.

Toshiyuki Takezawa, Eiichiro Sumita, Fumiaki Sugaya, Hirofumi Yamamoto, and Seiichi Yamamoto. 2002. Toward a broad-coverage bilingual corpus for speech translation of travel conversations in the real world. In *Proceedings of Third International Conference on Language Resources and Evaluation 2002*, pages 147–152, Las Palmas, Spain.

David Vilar, Maja Popovic, and Hermann Ney. 2006. AER: Do we need to "improve" our alignments? In *Proceedings of the International Workshop on Spoken Language Translation*, pages 205–212, Kyoto, Japan.

Stefan Vogel, Hermann Ney, and Christoph Tillmann. 1996. HMM-based word alignment in statistical translation. In *Proceedings of the 16th International Conference on Computational Linguistics*, pages 836–841, Copenhagen, Denmark.

Wei Wang and Ming Zhou. 2004. Improving word alignment models using structured monolingual corpora. In Dekang Lin and Dekai Wu, editors, *Proceedings of Conference on Empirical Methods in Natural Language Processing*, pages 198–205, Barcelona, Spain.

Dekai Wu. 1997. Stochastic Inversion Transduction Grammars and bilingual parsing of parallel corpora. *Computational Linguistics*, 23(3):377–403.

Inductive Detection of Language Features via Clustering Minimal Pairs: Toward Feature-Rich Grammars in Machine Translation

Jonathan H. Clark, Robert Frederking, Lori Levin
Language Technologies Institute
Carnegie Mellon University
Pittsburgh, PA 15213, USA
{jhclark,ref,lsl}@cs.cmu.edu

Abstract

Syntax-based Machine Translation systems have recently become a focus of research with much hope that they will outperform traditional Phrase-Based Statistical Machine Translation (PBSMT). Toward this goal, we present a method for analyzing the morphosyntactic content of language from an Elicitation Corpus such as the one included in the LDC's upcoming LCTL language packs. The presented method discovers a mapping between morphemes and linguistically relevant features. By providing this tool that can augment structure-based MT models with these rich features, we believe the discriminative power of current models can be improved. We conclude by outlining how the resulting output can then be used in inducing a morphosyntactically feature-rich grammar for AVENUE, a modern syntax-based MT system.

1 Introduction

Recent trends in Machine Translation have begun moving toward the incorporation of syntax and structure in translation models in hopes of gaining better translation quality. In fact, some structure-based systems have already shown that they can outperform phrase-based SMT systems (Chiang, 2005). Still, even the best-performing data-driven systems have not fully explored the depth of such linguistic features as morphosyntax.

Certainly, many have brought linguistically motivated features into their models in the past. Huang and Knight (2006) explored relabeling of non-terminal symbols to embed more information directly into the backbone of the grammar. Bonneau-Maynard et al. (2007) argue that incorporation of morphosyntax in the form of a part of speech (POS) language model can improve translation. While these approaches do make use of various linguistic features, we have only begun to scratch the surface of what actually occurs in the languages of the world. We wish to address such issues as case marking, subject-verb agreement, and numeral-classifier agreement by providing models with information about which morphemes correspond to which grammatical meanings.

2 Task Overview

Feature Detection is the process of determining from a corpus annotated with feature structures (Figure 2) which feature values (Figure 1) have a distinct representation in a target language in terms of morphemes (Figure 3). By leveraging knowledge from the field of language typology, we know what types of phenomena are possible across languages and, thus, which features to include in our feature specification.

But not every language will display each of these phenomena. Our goal is to determine which feature values (e.g. singular, dual, plural) have a distinct encoding in a given target language. Viewed differently, we can ask which feature values can be clustered by similarity. For instance, in Chinese, we would expect singular, plural and dual to be members of the same cluster (since they are typically not explicitly expressed), while for Arabic we should place each of these into separate clusters to indicate they are each grammaticalized differently. Similarly,

Proceedings of the Second ACL Workshop on Syntax and Structure in Statistical Translation (SSST-2), pages 78–86,
ACL-08: HLT, Columbus, Ohio, USA, June 2008.

Feature Name	Feature Value	Comment
np-gen	m ,f, n	Biological Gender
np-def	+, -	Definiteness
np-num	sg, dl, pl	Number
c-ten	past, pres, fut	Tense
np-function	act, und	Actor and undergoer participant roles
c-function	main, rel	Main and relative clause roles

Figure 1: An example feature specification.

ID	Source Language	Target Language	Lexical Cluster	Feature Structure
s1	He loves her.	El ama a ella.	$\ell 1$	((act (np-gen m) (np-num sg) (np-def +)) (und (np-gen f) (np-num sg) (np-def +)) (c-ten pres))
s2	She loves her.	Ella ama a ella.	$\ell 1$	((act (np-gen f) (np-num sg) (np-def +)) (und (np-gen f) (np-num sg) (np-def +)) (c-ten pres))
s3	He loved her.	El *ama a ella.	$\ell 1$	((act (np-gen m) (np-num sg) (np-def +)) (und (np-gen f) (np-num sg) (np-def +)) (c-ten past))
s4	The boy eats.	El niño come.	$\ell 2$	((act (np-gen m) (np-num sg) (np-def +)) (c-ten pres))
s5	The girl eats.	La niña come.	$\ell 2$	((act (np-gen f) (np-num sg) (np-def +)) (c-ten pres))
s6	A girl eats.	Una niña come.	$\ell 2$	((act (np-gen f) (np-num sg) (np-def -)) (c-ten pres))
s7	The girls eat.	Las niñas comen.	$\ell 2$	((act (np-gen f) (np-num pl) (np-def +)) (c-ten pres))
s8	The girls eat.	Las niñas comen.	$\ell 2$	((act (np-gen f) (np-num dl) (np-def +)) (c-ten pres))
s9	Girls eat.	Unas niñas comen.	$\ell 2$	((act (np-gen f) (np-num pl) (np-def -)) (c-ten pres))

Figure 2: An example of sentences that might be found in an elicitation corpus. Notice that each sentence differs from some other sentence in the corpus by exactly one feature value. This enables us to see how the written form of the language changes (or does not change) when the grammatical meaning changes.

English would have two clusters for the feature number: (singular) and (dual, plural). Further, we would like to determine which morphemes express each of these values (or value clusters). For example, English expresses negation with the morphemes *no* and *not*, whereas questions are expressed by reordering of the auxiliary verb or the addition of a wh-word.

Though many modern corpora contain feature-annotated utterances, these corpora are often not suitable for feature detection. For this purpose, we use an Elicitation Corpus (see Figure 2), a corpus that has been carefully constructed to provide a large number of *minimal pairs* of sentences such as *He sings* and *She sings* so that only a single feature (e.g. gender) differs between the two sentences. Also, notice that the feature structures are sometimes more detailed than the source language sentence. For example, English does not express dual number, but we might want to include this feature in our Elicitation Corpus (especially for a language such as Arabic). For these cases, we include a context field for the translator with an instruction such as "Translate this sentence as if there are two girls."

In the past, we proposed *deductive* (rule-based) methods for feature detection (Clark et al., 2008). In this paper, we propose the use of *inductive feature detection*, which operates directly on the feature set that the corpus has been annotated with, removing the need for manually written rules. We define inductive feature detection as a recall-oriented task since its output is intended to be analyzed by a Morphosyntactic Lexicon Generator, which will address the issue of precision. This, in turn, allows us to inform a rule learner about which language features can be clustered and handled by a single set of rules and which must be given special attention. However, due to the complexity of this component, describing it is beyond the scope of this paper. We also note that future work will include the integration of a morphology analysis system such as ParaMor (Monson et al., 2007) to extract and annotate the valuable morphosyntactic information of inflected languages. An example of this processing pipeline is given in Figure 4.

Feature	Value	Candidate Morphemes
np-gen	m	el, niño
np-gen	f	ella, niña
np-gen	n	*unobserved*
np-def	+	el, la, las
np-def	-	una, unas
np-num	sg	el, ella, la, una, come, niño, niña
np-num	dl-pl	las, unas, comen, niñas
c-ten	past-pres	–
c-ten	fut	*unobserved*

Figure 3: An example of the output of our system for the above corpus: a list of feature-morpheme pairings.

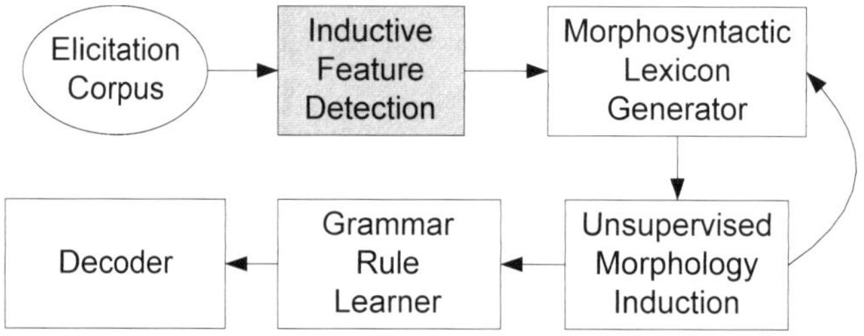

Figure 4: An outline of the steps from an input Elicitation Corpus to the application of a morphosyntactically feature rich grammar in a MT decoder. This paper discusses the highlighted *inductive feature detection* component. Note that this is just one possible configuration for integrating inductive feature detection into system training.

3 The Need to Observe Real Data

One might argue that such information could be obtained from a grammatical sketch of a language. However, these sketches often focus on the "interesting" features of a language, rather than those that are most important for machine translation. Further, not all grammatical functions are encoded in the elements that most grammatical sketches focus on. According to Construction Grammar, such information is also commonly found in *constructions* (Kay, 2002). For example, future tense is not grammaticalized in Japanese according to most reference sources, yet it may be expressed with a construction such as *watashi wa gakoo ni iku yode desu* (lit. *"I have a plan to go to school."*) for *I will go to school.* Feature detection informs us of such constructionalized encodings of language features for use in improving machine translation models.

Recognizing the need for this type of data, the LDC has included our Elicitation Corpus in their Less Commonly Taught Languages (LCTL) language packs (Simpson et al., 2008). Already, these language packs have been translated into Thai, Bengali, Urdu, Hungarian, Punjabi, Tamil, and Yoruba. With structured elicitation corpora already being produced on a wide scale, there exists plenty of data that can be exploited via feature detection. Some of these language packs have already been released for use in MT competitions and they will start being released to the general research community this year through LDC's catalog.

4 Applications

4.1 Induction of Feature-Rich Grammars

Given these outputs, a synchronous grammar induction system can then use these feature-annotated morphemes and the knowledge of which features are expressed to create a feature rich grammar. Consider the example in Figure 5, which shows Urdu subject-verb agreement taking place while being separated by 12 words. Traditional n-gram Language Models (LM's) would not be able to detect any disagreements more than n words away, which is the normal case for a trigram LM. Even most syntax-based systems would not be able to detect this problem without using a huge number of non-terminals, each marked for all possible agreements. A syntax-based system might be able to check this sort of agree-

ek	**talb**	alm	arshad	jo	mchhlyoN	ke liye	pani	maiN	aata	phink	**raha**	**tha** ...
a.SG	**student**	named	Irshad	who	fish	for	water	in	flour	throw	**PROG.SG.M**	**be.PAST.SG.M**

"A student named Irshad who was throwing flour in the water for the fish ..."

Figure 5: A glossed example from parallel text in LDC's Urdu-English LCTL language pack showing subject-verb agreement being separated by 12 words.

ment if it produced a target-side dependency tree as in Ding and Palmer (2005). However, we are not aware of any systems that attempt this. Therefore, the correct hypotheses, which have correct agreement, will likely be produces as hypotheses of traditional beam-search MT systems, but their features might not be able to discern the correct hypothesis, allowing it to fall below the 1-best or out of the beam entirely. By constructing a feature-rich grammar in a framework that allows unification-based feature constraints such as AVENUE (Carbonell et al., 2002), we can prune these bad hypotheses lacking agreement from the search space.

Returning to the example of subject-verb agreement, consider the following Urdu sentences taken from the Urdu-English Elicitation Corpus in LDC's LCTL language pack:

Danish	ne	Amna	ko	sza	di
Danish	ERG	Amna	DAT	punish	give.PERF

"Danish punished Amna."

Danish	Amna	ko	sza	dita	hai
Danish	Amna	DAT	punish	give.HAB	be.PRES

"Danish punishes Amna."

These examples show the split-ergativity of Urdu in which the ergative marker *ne* is used only for the subject of transitive, perfect aspect verbs. In particular, since these sentences have the perfect aspect marked on the light verb *di*, a closed-class word (Poornima and Koenig, 2008), feature detection will allow the induction of a grammar that percolates a feature up from the VP containing *di* indicating that its aspect is perfect. Likewise, the NP containing *Danish ne* will percolate a feature up indicating that the use of *ne* requires perfect aspect. If, during translation, a hypothesis is proposed that does not meet either of these conditions, unification will fail and the hypothesis will be pruned [1].

Certainly, unification-based grammars are not the only way in which this rich source of linguistic information could be used to augment a structure-based translation system. One could also imagine a system in which the feature annotations are simply used to improve the discriminative power of a model. For example, factored translation models (Koehn and Hoang, 2007) retain the simplicity of phrase-based SMT while adding the ability to incorporate additional features. Similarly, there exists a continuum of degrees to which this linguistic information can be used in current syntax-based MT systems. As modern systems move toward integrating many features (Liang et al., 2006), resources such as this will become increasingly important in improving translation quality.

5 System Description

In the following sections, we will describe the process of inductive feature detection by way of a running example.

5.1 Feature Specification

The first input to our system is a feature specification (Figure 1). The feature specification used for this experiment was written by an expert in language typology and is stored in a human-readable XML format. It is intended to cover a large number of phenomena that are possible in the languages of the world. Note that features beginning with `np-` are participant (noun) features while features beginning with `c-` are clause features. The feature specification allows us to know which values are unobserved during elicitation (that is, no sentence having that feature value was given to the bilingual person to translate). This is the case for the first four features and their values in Figure 1. The last two function features and their values tell us what possible roles participants and clauses can take in sentences.

[1] If the reader is not familiar with Unification Grammars, we recommend Kaplan (1995)

5.2 Elicitation Corpus

As outlined in Section 3, feature detection uses an Elicitation Corpus (see Figure 2), a corpus that has been carefully constructed to provide a large number of *minimal pairs* of sentences such as *He sings* and *She sings* so that only a single feature (e.g. gender) differs between the two sentences (Levin et al., 2006; Alvarez et al., 2006). If two features had varied at once (e.g. *It sang*) or lexical choice varied (e.g. *She reads*), then making assertions about which features the language does and does not express becomes much more difficult.

Notice that each input sentence has been tagged with an identifier for a *lexical cluster* as a pre-processing step. Specifying lexical clusters ensures that we don't compare sentences with different content just because their feature structures match. For example, we would not want to compare *Dog bites man* and *Man bites dog* nor *The student snored* and *The professor snored.* Note that bag-of-words matching is insufficient for this purpose.

Though any feature-annotated corpus can be used in feature detection, the amount of useful information extracted from the corpus is directly dependent on how many minimal pairs can be formed from the corpus. For instance, one might consider using a morphologically annotated corpus or even an automatically parsed corpus in place of the elicitation corpus. Even though these resources are likely to suffer from having very sparse minimal pairs due to their uncontrolled usage of vocabulary, they might still contain some amount of useful information. However, since we seek both to apply these methods to language for which there are currently no manually annotated corpora and to investigate features that existing parsers generally cannot identify (e.g. generic nouns and evidentiality), we will not mention these types of resources any further.

5.3 Minimal Pair Clustering

Minimal pair clustering is the process of grouping all possible sets of minimal pairs, those pairs of sentences that have exactly one difference between their feature structures. We use *wildcard feature structures* to represent each minimal pair cluster. We define a *wildcard feature* as any feature whose value is *, which denotes that the value matches another * rather than its original feature value. Similarly, we define the *feature context* of the wildcard feature be the enclosing participant and clause type for a `np-` feature or the enclosing clause for a `c-` type feature. Then, for each sentence s in the corpus, we substitute a wildcard feature for each of the values v in its feature structure, and we append s to the list of sentences associated with this wildcard feature structure. A sample of some of the minimal pairs for our running example are shown in Figure 6.

Here, we show minimal pairs for just one wildcard, though multiple wildcards may be created if one wishes to examine how features interact with one another. This could be useful in cases such as Hindi where the perfective verb aspect interacts with the past verb tense and the actor NP function to add the case marker *ne* (for split ergativity of Urdu, see Section 4.1). That said, a downstream component such as a Morphosyntactic Lexicon Generator would perhaps be better suited for the analysis of feature interactions. Also, note that the feature context is not used when there is only one wildcard feature. The feature context becomes useful when multiple wildcards are added in that it may also act as a wildcard feature.

The next step is to organize the example sentences into a table that helps us decide which examples can be compared and stores information that will inform our comparison. Briefly, any two sentences belonging to the same minimal pair cluster and lexical cluster will eventually get compared. As specified in Algorithm 1, we create a table like that in Figure 7. Having collected this information, we are now ready to begin clustering feature values.

Algorithm 1 Organize()

Require: Minimal pairs, lexical clusters, and the feature specification.
Ensure: A table T of comparable examples.
  for all pair $m \in$ minimalPairs **do**
    for all sentence $s \in$ m **do**
      f ← wildcardFeature(s, m)
      v ← featureValue(s, f)
      c ← featureContext(m)
      ℓ ← lexCluster(s)
      $\text{T}[f, m, c, \ell, v] \leftarrow \text{T}[f, m, c, \ell, v] \cup \text{s}$
  return T

ID	Set Members	Feature	Feature Context	Feature Structure
m1	{s1, s2}	np-gen	((act))	((act (np-gen *) (np-num sg) (np-def +)) (und (np-gen f) (np-num sg) (np-def +)) (c-ten pres))
m2	{s1, s3}	np-ten	()	((act (np-gen m) (np-num sg) (np-def +)) (und (np-gen f) (np-num sg) (np-def +)) (c-ten *))
m3	{s4, s5, s7, s8}	np-gen	((act))	((act (np-gen *) (np-num sg) (np-def +)) (c-ten pres))
m4	{s5, s7, s8}	np-num	((act))	((act (np-gen f) (np-num *) (np-def +)) (c-ten pres))
m5	{s6, s9}	np-num	((act))	((act (np-gen f) (np-num *) (np-def -)) (c-ten pres))
m6	{s5, s6}	np-def	((act))	((act (np-gen f) (np-num sg) (np-def *)) (c-ten pres))
m7	{s7, s9}	np-def	((act))	((act (np-gen f) (np-num pl) (np-def *)) (c-ten pres))

Figure 6: An example subset of minimal pairs that can be formed from the corpus in Figure 2.

Feature	Min. Pair	Feat. Context	Lex. Cluster	Feat. Value.	Sentence
np-gen	m1	((act))	$\ell 1$	m	s1
np-gen	m1	((act))	$\ell 1$	f	s2
np-ten	m2	()	$\ell 1$	pres	s1
np-ten	m2	()	$\ell 1$	past	s3
np-num	m4	((act))	$\ell 2$	sg	s5
np-num	m4	((act))	$\ell 2$	pl	s7
np-num	m4	((act))	$\ell 2$	dl	s8
np-num	m5	((act))	$\ell 2$	sg	s6
np-num	m5	((act))	$\ell 2$	pl	s9

Figure 7: An example subset of the organized items that can be formed from the minimal pairs in Figure 6. Each item that has a matching minimal pair ID, feature context, and lexical cluster ID can be compared during feature detection.

5.4 Feature Value Clustering

During the process of feature value clustering, we collapse feature values that do not have a distinct encoding in the target language into a single group. This is helpful both as information to components using the output of inductive feature detection and later as a method of reducing data sparseness when creating morpheme-feature pairings. We represent the relationship between the examples we have gathered for each feature as a *feature expression graph.* We define a feature expression graph (FEG) for a feature f to be a graph on $|v|$ vertices where v is the number of possible values of f (though for most non-trivial cases, it is more conveniently represented as a triangular matrix).

Each vertex of the FEG corresponds to a feature value (e.g. singular, dual) while each arc contains the list of examples that are comparable according to the table from the previous step. The examples at each arc are organized into those that had the same target language string, indicating that the feature values are not distinctly expressed, and those that had a different target language string, indicating that the change in grammatical meaning represented in the feature structure has a distinct encoding in the target language. Algorithm 2 more formally specifies the creation of a FEG. The FEG's for our running example are shown in Figure 8. From these statistics generated from these graphs, we then estimate the maximum likelihood probability of each feature value pair being distinctly encoded as shown in Figure 9.

The interpretation of these probabilities might not be obvious. They estimate the likelihood of a language encoding a feature given that the meaning of that feature is intended to be conveyed. These probabilities should *not* be interpreted as a traditional likelihood of encountering a given lexical item.

Finally, we cluster by randomly selecting a starting vertex for a new cluster and adding vertices to that cluster, following arcs out from the cluster that have a weight lower than some threshold θ. When no more arcs may be followed, a new start vertex is selected and another cluster is formed. This is repeated until all feature values have been assigned to a cluster. For our running example, we use $\theta = 0.6$,

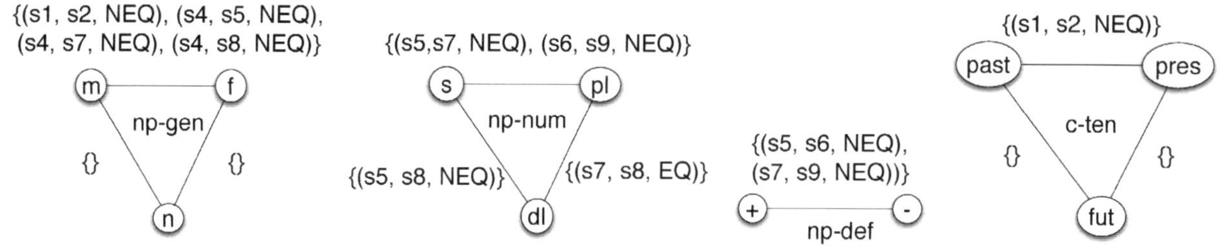

Figure 8: An example subset of the Feature Expression Graphs that are formed from the minimal pairs in Figure 7.

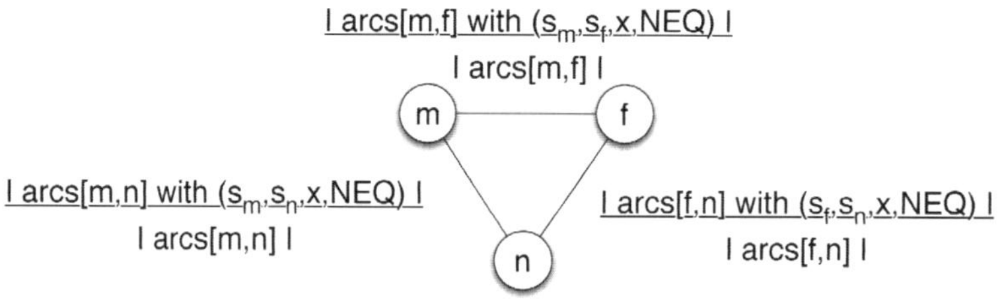

Figure 9: An example of how probabilities are estimated for each feature value pair in a Feature Expression Graph for the feature `np-gender`.

Algorithm 2 Collecting statistics for each FEG.

Require: The table T from the previous step.

Ensure: A complete graph as an arc list with the observed similarities and differences for each feature value.

  for all $s_i, s_j \in$ T s.t. $(m_i, c_i, \ell_i) = (m_j, c_j, \ell_j)$ **do**

    $(v_i, v_j) \leftarrow$ (featureValue(s_i), featureValue(s_j))

    if tgt(s_i) = tgt(s_j) **then**

      arcs$[v_i, v_j] \leftarrow$ arcs$[v_i, v_j] \cup (s_i, s_j, m,$EQ)

    else

      arcs$[v_i, v_j] \leftarrow$ arcs$[v_i, v_j] \cup (s_i, s_j, m,$NEQ)

  return arcs

which results in the following clusters being formed:

```
np-gen: m, f
np-num: s, pl/dl
np-def: +, -
c-ten: past, pres
```

5.5 Morpheme-Feature Pairing

Finally, using the information from above about which values should be examined as a group and which sentence pairs exemplify an orthographic difference, we examine each pair of target language sentences to determine which words changed to reflect the change in grammatical meaning. This process is outlined in Algorithm 3. The general idea is that for each arc going out of a feature value vertex we examine all of the target language sentence pairs that expressed a difference. We then take the words that were in the vocabulary of the target sentence for the current feature value, but not in the sentence it was being compared to and add them to the list of words that could be used to express this feature value (Figure 3).

6 Evaluation and Results

We evaluated the output of feature detection with one wildcard feature as applied to the Elicitation Corpus from the LDC's Urdu-English LCTL language pack. Threshold parameters were set to small values ($\theta = 0.05$). Note that an increase in precision might be possible by tuning this value; however, as stated, we are most concerned with recall.

An initial attempt was made to create a gold standard against which recall could be directly calculated. However, the construction of this gold standard was both noisier and more time consuming than expected. That is, even though the task is based on how a linguistic field worker might col-

Algorithm 3 Determine which morphemes are associated with which feature values.

Require: List of clusters C and list of FEGs F
Ensure: A list of morphemes associated with each feature value

- **for all** feature $\in$ F **do**
  - **for all** vertex $\in$ feature **do**
    - **for all** arc $\in$ vertex **do**
      - **for all** $(s_1, s_2, m,$NEQ$)$ $\in$ arc **do**
        - $v_1 \leftarrow$ featureValue(s_1,m)
        - $v_2 \leftarrow$ featureValue(s_2,m)
        - **if** $v_1 \neq v$ **then** $(s_1, v_1) \leftrightarrow (s_2, v_2)$
        - $w_1 \leftarrow$ vocabulary(s_1)
        - $w_2 \leftarrow$ vocabulary(s_2)
        - $\delta \leftarrow W_1 - W_2$
        - **for all** w $\in$ freq **do**
          - freq$[w]$++
      - **for all** w $\in$ freq **do**
        - p = freq$[w]$ / Σ_w freq$[w]$
        - **if** $p \geq \theta'$ **then**
          - morphemes$[v]$ $\leftarrow$ morphemes$[v]\cup$ w
- **return** morphemes

lect data, it was more difficult for a human than anticipated. Therefore, we instead produced a list of hypothesized morpheme-feature pairs and had a human trained in linguistics who was also bilingual in Hindi/Urdu-English mark each pair as "Correct," "Incorrect," or "Ambiguous." The results of this evaluation are summarized in Figure 10. The reader may be surprised by how many incorrect hypotheses were generated, given the controlled nature of the Elicitation Corpus. However, there are two important factors to consider. First, features can interact in complex and often unexpected ways. For instance, in English, the only feature difference in minimal pair *Cats yawned* and *A cat yawned* is the number of the actor. However, this causes an interaction with definiteness that would cause the presented algorithms to associate *a* with the number of nouns even though it is canonically associated with definiteness. Second, the bilingual people translating the Elicitation Corpus are prone to make errors.

Though a fair number of incorrect hypotheses were produced, the number of correct hypotheses is encouraging. We also note that the words being identified are largely function words and multi-

Judgment	Morpheme-Feature Pairings
Correct	68
Ambiguous	29
Incorrect	109
TOTAL	206

Figure 10: The results of feature detection. Being a recall-oriented approach, inductive feature detection is geared toward overproduction of morpheme-feature pairings as shown in the number of ambiguous and incorrect pairings.

morpheme tokens from which closed-class functional morphemes will be extracted. One might think the counts extracted seem low when compared to the typical MT vocabulary size, but these function words that we extract cover a much larger probability mass of the language than content words.

We are confident that the Morphosyntactic Lexicon Generator designed to operate directly downstream from this process will be sufficiently discriminant to use these morpheme-feature pairings to create a high precision lexicon. However, since this component is, in itself, highly complex, its specifics are beyond the scope of this paper and so we leave it to be discussed in future work.

7 Conclusion

We have presented a method for inductive feature detection of an annotated corpus, which determines which feature values have a distinct representation in a target language and what morphemes can be used to express these grammatical meanings. This method exploits the unique properties of an Elicitation Corpus, a resource which is becoming widely available from the LDC. Finally, we have argued that the output of feature detection is useful for exploiting these linguistic features via a feature-rich grammar for a machine translation system.

Acknowledgments

We would like to thank our colleagues Alon Lavie, Vamshi Ambati, Abhaya Agarwal, and Alok Parlikar for their insights. Thanks to Keisuke Kamataki for the Japanese example and to Shakthi Poornima for her help with the Urdu examples. This work was supported by US NSF Grant Number 0713-292.

References

Alison Alvarez, Lori Levin, Robert Frederking, Simon Fung, Donna Gates, and Jeff Good. 2006. The MILE corpus for less commonly taught languages. In *HLT-NAACL*, New York, New York, June.

H. Bonneau-Maynard, A. Allauzen, D. Déchelotte, and H. Schwenk. 2007. Combining morphosyntactic enriched representation with n-best reranking in statistical translation. In *Proceedings of the Workshop on Structure and Syntax in Statistical Translation (SSST) at NAACL-HLT*.

Jaime Carbonell, Kathrina Probst, Erik Peterson, Christian Monson, Alon Lavie, Ralf Brown, and Lori Levin. 2002. Automatic rule learning for resource limited MT. In *Association for Machine Translation in the Americas (AMTA)*, October.

David Chiang. 2005. A hierarchical phrase-based model for statistical machine translation. In *Association for Computational Linguistics (ACL)*.

Jonathan H. Clark, Robert Frederking, and Lori Levin. 2008. Toward active learning in corpus creation: Automatic discovery of language features during elicitation. In *Proceedings of the Language Resources and Evaluation Conference (LREC)*.

Yuan Ding and Martha Palmer. 2005. Machine translation using probabilistic synchronous dependency insertion grammars. In *Proceedings of the 43rd Meeting of the Association for Computational Linguistics ACL*.

Bryant Huang and Kevin Knight. 2006. Relabeling syntax trees to improve syntax-based machine translation quality. In *Proceedings of (NAACL-HLT)*.

Ronald Kaplan. 1995. The formal architecture of lexical functional grammar. In Mary Dalrymple, Ronald Kaplan, J. Maxwell, and A. Zaenen, editors, *Formal Issues in Lexical Functional Grammar*. CSLI Publications.

Paul Kay. 2002. An informal sketch of a formal architecture for construction grammar. In *Grammars*.

Phillipp Koehn and Hieu Hoang. 2007. Factored translation models. In *Empirical Methods in Natural Language Processing (EMNLP)*.

Lori Levin, Jeff Good, Alison Alvarez, and Robert Frederking. 2006. Parallel reverse treebanks for the discovery of morpho-syntactic markings. In *Proceedings of Treebanks and Linguistic Theory*, Prague.

Percy Liang, Alexandre Bouchard-Cote, Dan Klein, and Ben Taskar. 2006. An end-to-end discriminative approach to machine translation. In *Proceedings of the 44th Annual Meeting of the Association for Computational Linguistics*, Sydney.

Christian Monson, Jaime Carbonell, Alon Lavie, and Lori Levin. 2007. Paramor: Minimally supervised induction of paradigm structure and morphological analysis. In *Proceedings of the 9th ACL SIGMORPH*.

Shakthi Poornima and Jean-Pierre Koenig. 2008. Reverse complex predicates in Hindi. In *Proceedings of the 24th Northwest Linguistic Conference*.

Heather Simpson, Christopher Cieri, Kazuaki Maeda, Kathryn Baker, and Boyan Onyshkevych. 2008. Human language technology resources for less commonly taught languages: Lessons learned toward creation of basic language resources. In *Proceedings of the LREC 2008 Workshop on Collaboration: interoperability between people in the creation of language resources for less-resourced langauges*.

Syntax-driven Learning of Sub-sentential Translation Equivalents and Translation Rules from Parsed Parallel Corpora

Alon Lavie
alavie@cs.cmu.edu
Language Technologies Institute
Carnegie Mellon University
Pittsburgh, PA 15213, USA

Alok Parlikar
aup@cs.cmu.edu
Language Technologies Institute
Carnegie Mellon University
Pittsburgh, PA 15213, USA

Vamshi Ambati
vambati@cs.cmu.edu
Language Technologies Institute
Carnegie Mellon University
Pittsburgh, PA 15213, USA

Abstract

We describe a multi-step process for automatically learning reliable sub-sentential syntactic phrases that are translation equivalents of each other and syntactic translation rules between two languages. The input to the process is a corpus of parallel sentences, word-aligned and annotated with phrase-structure parse trees. We first apply a newly developed algorithm for aligning parse-tree nodes between the two parallel trees. Next, we extract all aligned sub-sentential syntactic constituents from the parallel sentences, and create a syntax-based phrase-table. Finally, we treat the node alignments as tree decomposition points and extract from the corpus all possible synchronous parallel tree fragments. These are then converted into synchronous context-free rules. We describe the approach and analyze its application to Chinese-English parallel data.

1 Introduction

Phrase-based Statistical MT (PB-SMT) (Koehn et al., 2003) has become the predominant approach to Machine Translation in recent years. PB-SMT requires broad-coverage databases of phrase-to-phrase translation equivalents. These are commonly acquired from large volumes of automatically word-aligned sentence-parallel text corpora. Accurate identification of sub-sentential translation equivalents, however, is a critical process in all data-driven MT approaches, including a variety of data-driven syntax-based approaches that have been developed in recent years. (Chiang, 2005) (Imamura et al., 2004) (Galley et al., 2004).

In this paper, we describe a multi-step process for automatically learning reliable sub-sentential syntactic phrases that are translation equivalents of each other and syntactic translation rules between two languages. The input to the process is a corpus of parallel sentences, word-aligned and annotated with phrase-structure parse trees for both languages. Our method consists of three steps. In the first step, we apply a newly developed algorithm for aligning parse-tree nodes between the two parallel trees. In the second step, we extract all aligned sub-sentential syntactic constituents from the parallel sentences, and create a syntax-based phrase-table. Our syntactic phrases come with constituent "labels" which can guide their syntactic function during decoding. In the final step, we treat the node alignments as tree decomposition points and extract from the corpus all possible synchronous parallel tree fragments. These are then converted into synchronous context-free rules. Our methods do not depend on any specific properties of the underlying phrase-structure representations or the parsers used, and were designed to be applicable even when these representations are quite different for the two languages.

The approach described is used to acquire the resources for a statistical syntax-based MT approach that we have developed (Stat-XFER), briefly described below. The resulting resources can, however, be used in any syntax-based data-driven MT approach other than our own. The focus of this paper is on our syntax-driven process for extracting phrases and rules from data. We describe the approach and analyze its effectiveness when applied to large-volumes of Chinese-English parallel data.

Proceedings of the Second ACL Workshop on Syntax and Structure in Statistical Translation (SSST-2), pages 87–95,
ACL-08: HLT, Columbus, Ohio, USA, June 2008.

1.1 The Stat-XFER MT Framework

Stat-XFER is a search-based syntax-driven framework for building MT systems. The underlying formalism is based on synchronous context-free grammars. The synchronous rules can optionally be augmented by unification-style feature constraints. The synchronous grammars can be acquired automatically from data, but also manually developed by experts. A simple example transfer-rule (for Chinese-to-English) can be seen below:

```
{NP,1062753}
NP::NP [DNP NP] -> [NP PP]
(
(*score* 0.946640316205534)
(X2::Y1)
(X1::Y2)
)
```

Each rule has a unique identifier followed by a synchronous rule for both source and target sides. The alignment of source-to-target constituents is explicitly represented using 'X' indices for the source side, and 'Y' indices for the target side. Rules can also have lexical items on either side, in which case no alignment information is required for these elements. Feature constraints can optionally be specified for both source and target elements of the rule. We do not address the learning of feature constraints in the work described here, and concentrate only on the acquisition of the synchronous CFG rules. The rules can be modeled statistically and assigned scores, which can then be used as decoding features.

The Stat-XFER framework also includes a fully-implemented transfer engine that applies the transfer grammar to a source-language input sentence at runtime, and produces collections of scored word and phrase-level translations according to the grammar. These are collected into a lattice data-structure. Scores are based on a log-linear combination of several features, and a beam-search controls the underlying parsing and transfer process. A second-stage monotonic decoder is responsible for combining translation fragments into complete translation hypotheses (Lavie, 2008)

2 PFA Algorithm for Node Aligment

2.1 Objectives of the Algorithm

Our objective of the first stage of our approach is to detect sub-sentential constituent correspondences in parallel sentences, based on phrase-structure parses for the two corresponding sentences. Given a pair of parallel sentences and their corresponding parse trees, our goal is to find pairings of nodes in the source and target trees whose yields are translation equivalents of each other. Our current approach only considers complete constituents and their contigious yields, and will therefore not align discontiguous phrases or partial constituents. Similar to phrase extraction methods in PB-SMT, we rely on word-level alignments (derived manually or automatically) as indicators for translation equivalence. The assumption applied is that if two words are aligned with each other, they carry the same meaning and can be treated as translation equivalents. Constituents are treated as compositional units of meaning and translation equivalence.

2.2 Related Work

Aligning nodes in parallel trees has been investigated by a number of previous researchers. (Samuelsson and Volk, 2007) describe a process for manual alignment of nodes in parallel trees. This approach is well suited for generating reliable parallel treebanks, but is impractical for accumulating resources from large parallel data. (Tinsley et al., 2007) use statistical lexicons derived from automatic statistical word alignment for aligning nodes in parallel trees. In our approach, we use the word alignment information directly, which we believe may be more reliable than the statistical lexicon. (Groves et al., 2004) propose a method of aligning nodes between parallel trees automatically, based on word alignments. In addition to the word alignment information, their approach uses the constituent labels of nodes in the trees, and the general structure of the tree. Our approach is more general in the sense that we only consider the word alignments, thereby making the approach applicable to any parser or phrase-structure representation, even ones that are quite different for the two languages involved.

2.3 Unaligned Words and Contiguity

Word-level alignment of phrase-level translation equivalents often leaves some words unaligned. For example, some languages have articles, while others do not. It is thus reasonable to expect that constituent pairs in parallel trees that are good translation equivalents of each other may contain some unaligned words. Our PFA node-alignment algorithm allows for such constituents to be matched.

Different languages have different word orders. In English, an adjective always comes before a noun, while in French, in most cases, the adjective follows its noun. Our node alignment algorithm allows aligning of constituents regardless of the word order expressed by the linear precedence relation of their sub-constituents. As long as one piece of contiguous text dominated by a node covers the same word-level alignments as the yield of a node in the parallel tree, the two nodes can be aligned.

2.4 Wellformedness constraints

Given a pair of word-aligned sentences and their corresponding parse trees S and T, represented as sets of constituent nodes, our PFA node alignment algorithm produces a collection of aligned node-pairs (S_i, T_j). The underlying assumptions of compositionality in meaning and word-level alignments being indicative of translation equivalence lead directly to the following node alignment wellformedness criteria:

1. If a node S_i is linked to a node T_j, then any node within the subtree of node S_i can only be linked to nodes within the subtree of node T_j.

2. If a node S_i is linked to a node T_j, then any node that dominates the node S_i can only be linked to nodes that dominate the node T_j.

3. If a node S_i is linked to a node T_j, then the word alignments of the yields of the two constituents must satisfy the following:
   (a) Every word in the yield of the node S_i must be aligned to one or more words in the yield of the node T_j, or it should be unaligned.
   (b) Every word in the yield of the node T_j must be aligned to one or more words in the yield of the node S_i, or it should be unaligned.
   (c) There should be at least one alignment between the yields of nodes S_i and T_j. Thus, the words in the yields can not all be unaligned.

2.5 Arithmetic Representation

Our PFA algorithm uses a arithmetic mapping that elegently carries over the constraints characterized by the wellformedness constraints elaborated above. This mapping is designed to ensure that each aligned word, which carries a distinct "piece of meaning" can be uniquely identified, and also inherently reflects the compositional properties of constituent translation equivalence. This is accomplished by assigning numerical values to the nodes of the two parse trees being aligned, in a bottom-up fashion, starting from the leaf nodes of the trees. Leaf nodes that correspond to words that are aligned are each assigned a unique prime number. Unaligned leaf nodes are assigned a value of "1". Constituent nodes in the parse trees are then assigned a value that is the product of all its sub-constituent nodes. Because of the arithmetic property that any composite number can be uniquely factored into primes, it should be evident that the value of every constituent node uniquely identifies the aligned words that are covered by its yield. Consequently, by assigning *the same* prime values to the aligned words of both trees, retrieving aligned constituent nodes is as simple as finding the set of nodes in the two trees that carry the same numerical value. Note that by assigning values of "1" to unaligned words, these unaligned words do not influence the numerical values assigned to constituent nodes, thus reflecting their treatment as "don't cares" with respect to the translation equivalence of constituent nodes.

2.6 Description of the PFA Algorithm

The PFA algorithm uses the concept of 'composite meaning as prime factorization', and hence the name (Prime Factorization and Alignments). The algorithm assigns values to the leaf nodes, propogates the values up the tree, and then compares the node values across the trees to align the nodes. As described above, leaf nodes which have word alignments are assigned unique prime numbers, and the

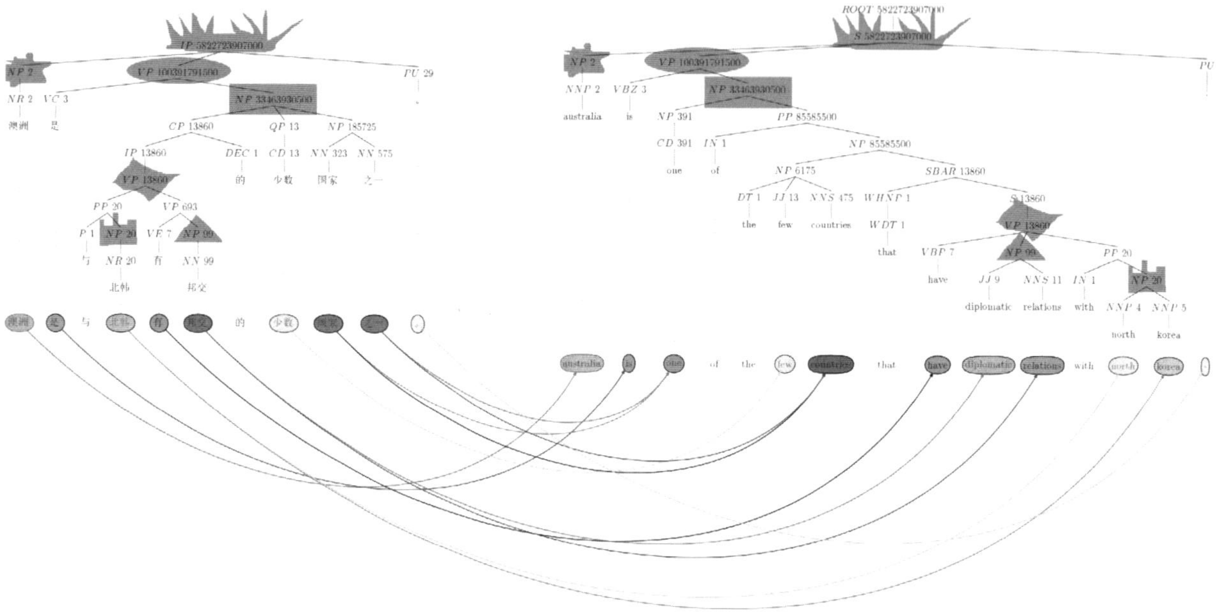

Figure 1: Node-Aligned Parallel Sentences

same prime is assigned to the corresponding aligned words in the parallel sentences. Leaf nodes corresponding to unaligned words are assigned the value "1". The treatment of "one-to-many" word alignments is a special case. Such alignments are considered to carry the same meaning, and should thus be assigned the same value. To accomplish this, if a single word is aligned to multiple words in the other language, we assign the same prime number to all words on the "multiple" side, and assign the product of these to the single word equivalent.

Another special case is when the parse trees contain unary productions. In this case, the values of both nodes involved in this production are the same. Our node alignment algorithm breaks this "tie" by selecting the node that is "lower" in the tree (the daughter node of the unary production). A similar situation with two nodes being assigned identical values can arise when one or more unaligned words are attached directly to the parent node. Here too, our algorithm aligns the "lower" node and leaves the "higher" node unaligned. These decisions reflect our desire to be conservative with respect to such ambiguous cases, and their implications on the notion of translational equivalence. This also provides some robustness against noisy alignments.

It is straightfoward to verify that the PFA algorithm satisfies the wellformedness constraints described above. Also, since multiplication is commutative, the algorithm is not effected by differing word orders within parallel constituent structures.

The PFA algorithm run on a sample Chinese-English parallel sentence is shown in Figure 1. The value of each node as shown as a part of its label. The aligned nodes are marked by shapes. A triangle aligns to a triangle, and squares to squares.

3 Syntax-based Sub-sentential Phrase Extraction

The alignment of nodes as described in the previous section allows us to build a comprehensive syntax-based phrase-to-phrase translation lexicon from a parallel corpus. To build a syntax-based "phrase table", we simply extract all aligned constituent nodes along with their yields and enter them into a database, while accumulating frequency counts. In addition to the source-to-target phrase correspondences, we record the constituent labels of the aligned constituent nodes on both the source and target sides (which may be different). These labels "connect" the phrases with synatactic transfer rules during decoding. The set of phrases extracted from the example sentence in Figure 1 is shown in Figure 2.

Source Category	Target Category	Source	Target
IP	S	澳洲 是 与 北韩 有 邦交 的 少数 国家 之一 。	Australia is one of the few countries that have diplomatic relations with North Korea.
VP	VP	是 与 北韩 有 邦交 的 少数 国家 之一	is one of the few countries that have diplomatic relations with North Korea
NP	NP	与 北韩 有 邦交 的 少数 国家 之一	one of the few countries that have diplomatic relations with North Korea
VP	VP	与 北韩 有 邦交	have diplomatic relations with North Korea
NP	NP	邦交	diplomatic relations
NP	NP	北韩	North Korea
NP	NP	澳洲	Australia

Figure 2: Phrases extracted from Aligned Nodes

The process of building syntax-based "phrase tables" from large corpora of sentence-parallel data is quite similar to the corresponding process in phrase-based SMT systems. Our phrase correspondences, however, only reflect contiguous and complete constituent correspondences. We also note that the extracted phrase tables in both approaches can be modeled statistically in similar ways. Similar to common practice in PB-SMT, we currently use the frequency counts of the phrases to calculate relative likelihood estimates and use these as features in our Stat-XFER decoder.

4 Evaluation of the PFA algorithm

The accuracy of our node alignment algorithm depends on both the quality of the word alignments as well as the accuracy of the parse trees. We performed several experiments to assess the effects of these underlying resources on the accuracy of our approach. The most accurate condition is when the parallel sentences are manually word-aligned, and when verified correct parse trees are available for both source and target sentences. Performance is expected to degrade when word alignments are produced using automatic methods, and when correct parse trees are replaced with automatic parser output. In these experiments, we used a manually word-aligned parallel Chinese-English TreeBank consisting of 3342 parallel sentences.

4.1 Manual Constituent Node Alignments

We first investigated the accuracy of our approach under the most accurate condition. We sampled 30 sentences from the Chinese-English treebank corpus. A bilingual expert from our group then manually aligned the nodes in these trees. These node alignments were then used as a "gold standard". We then used the accurate parse trees and the manually created word alignments for these sentence pairs, and ran the PFA node algorithm, and compared the resulting node alignments with the gold standard alignments. The Precision, Recall, F-1 and F-0.5 results are reported in Table 1.

Precision	Recall	F-1	F-0.5
0.8129	0.7325	0.7705	0.7841

Table 1: Accuracy of PFA Node Alignments against Manual Node Alignments

We manually inspected cases where there was a mismatch between the manual and automatic node alignments, and found several trends. Many of the alignment differences were the result of one-to-many or many-to-many word alignemnts. For example, in some cases a verb in Chinese was word-aligned to an auxiliary and a head verb on the english side (e.g. `have` and `put`). The PFA algorithm in this case node-aligns the `VP` that governs the Chinese verb to the `VP` that contains both auxiliary and head verbs on the English side. The gold standard human alignments, however, in some cases, aligned the `VP` of the Chinese verb to the English `VP` that governs just the main verb. Other mismatches were attributed to errors or inconsistencies in the manual word alignment and to the treatment of traces and fillers in the parse trees.

4.2 Effect of Using Automatic Word Alignments

We next tested how sensitive the PFA algorithm is to errors in automatic word alignment. We use the entire 3342 sentences in the parallel treebank for this experiment. We first ran the algorithm with the correct parse trees and manual word-alignments as input. We use the resulting node alignments as the gold standard in this case. We then used GIZA++ to get bidirectional word alignments, and combined them using various strategies. In this scenario, the trees are high-quality (from the treebank), but the alignments are noisy. The results obtained are shown in Table 2. Unsurprisingly, the "Union" combination method has the best precision but worst recall, while the "Intersection" combination method has the best recall but worst precision. The four

Comb Method	Prec	Rec	F-1	F-0.5
Intersection	0.6382	0.5395	0.5846	0.6014
Union	0.8114	0.2915	0.4288	0.5087
Sym1	0.7142	0.4534	0.5546	0.5992
Sym2	0.7135	0.4631	0.5616	0.6045
Grow-Diag-Final	0.7777	0.3462	0.4790	0.5493
Grw-Diag-Fin-And	0.6988	0.4700	0.5619	0.6011

Table 2: Manual Trees, Automatic Node Alignments

other methods for combining word alignments fall in between. Three of the four (all except "grow-diag-final") behave quite similarly. We generally believe that precision is somewhat more important than recall for this task, and have thus used the "sym2" method (Ortiz-Martínez et al., 2005) (which has the best F-0.5 score) for our translation experiments.

4.3 Effect of Using Automatic Parses

We evaluated the effect of parsing errors (as reflected in automatically derived parse trees) on the quality of the node alignments. We parsed the treebank corpus on both English and Chinese using the Stanford parser, and extracted phrases using manual word alignments. Compared to the phrases extracted from the manual trees, we obtained a precision of 0.8749, and a recall of 0.7227, that is, an F-0.5 measure of 0.8174. We then evaluated the most 'noisy' condition that involves both automatic word alignments and automatic parse trees. We evaluated the phrase extraction with different Viterbi combination strategies. The 'sym2' combination gave the best results, with a precision of 0.6251, recall of 0.3566, thus an F-0.5 measure of 0.4996.

5 Synchronous Tree Fragment and CFG Rule Extraction

5.1 Related Work

Syntax-based reordering rules can be used as a preprocessing step for PB-SMT (and other approaches), to decrease the word-order and syntactic distortion between the source and target languages (Xia and McCord, 2004). A variety of hierarchical and syntax-based models, which are applied during decoding, have also been developed. Many of these approaches involve automatic learning and extraction of the underlying syntax-based rules from data. The underlying formalisms used has been quite broad and include simple formalisms such as ITGs (Wu, 1997), hierarchical synchronous rules (Chiang, 2005), string to tree models by (Galley et al., 2004) and (Galley et al., 2006), synchronous CFG models such (Xia and McCord, 2004) (Yamada and Knight, 2001), synchronous Lexical Functional Grammar inspired approaches (Probst et al., 2002) and others.

Most of the previous approaches for acquiring syntactic transfer or reordering rules from parallel corpora use syntactic information from only one side of the parallel corpus, typically the target side. (Hearne and Way, 2003) describes an approach that uses syntactic information from the source side to derive reordering subtrees, which can then be used within a "data-oriented translation" (DOT) MT system, similar in framework to (Poutsma, 2000). Our work is different from the above in that we use syntactic trees for both source and target sides to infer constituent node alignments, from which we then learn synchronous trees and rules. Our process of extraction of rules as synchronous trees and then converting them to synchronous CFG rules is most similar to that of (Galley et al., 2004).

5.2 Synchronous Tree Fragment Pair Extraction

The main concept underlying our syntactic rule extraction process is that we treat the node alignments discovered by the PFA algorithm (described in previous sections) as synchronous tree decomposition points. This reflects the fact that these nodes denote points in the synchronous parse trees where translation correspondences can be put together compositionally. Using the aligned nodes as decomposition points, we break apart the synchronous trees into collections of minimal synchronous tree fragments. Finally, the synchronous fragments are also converted into synchronous context-free rules. These are then collected into a database of synchronous rules.

The input to our rule extraction process consists of the parallel parse trees along with their node alignment information. The constituent nodes in the parallel trees that were aligned by the PFA node alignment algorithm are treated as tree decomposition points. At each such decomposition point, spliting the two parallel trees results in two partial trees or tree fragments. One synchronous pair consists of the subtrees that are headed by the aligned nodes where the decomposition took place. Since the subtrees are rooted at aligned nodes, their yields are translation equivalents of each other. The other synchronous tree fragment pair consists of the remaining portions of the trees. The translation equivalence of the complete tree (or subtree) prior to decomposition implies that these tree fragments (which exclude the detached subtrees) also correspond to translation equivalents. The tree fragments that are obtained by decomposing the synchronous trees in this fashion are similar to the Synchronous Tree Insertion Grammar of (Shieber and Schabes, 1990).

We developed a tree traversal algorithm that decomposes parallel trees into all minimal tree fragments. Given two synchronous trees and their node alignment decomposition information, our tree fragment extraction algorithm operates by an "in-order" traversal of the trees top down, starting from the root nodes. The traversal can be guided by either the source or target parse tree. Each node in the tree that is marked as an aligned node triggers a decomposition. The subtree that is rooted at this node is removed from the currently traversed tree. A copy of the removed subtree is then recursively processed for top-down decomposition. If the current tree node being explored is not an aligned node (and thus is not a decomposition point), the traversal continues down the tree, possibly all the way to the leaves of the tree. Decomposition is performed on the corresponding parallel tree at the same time. We apply this process on all the aligned constituent nodes (decomposition points) to obtain all possible decomposed synchronous tree fragment pairs from the original parallel parse trees. This results in a collection of all minimal synchronous subtree fragments. These synchronous subtree fragments are minimal in the sense that they do not contain any internal aligned nodes. Another property of the synchronous subtree fragments is that their frontier nodes are either aligned nodes from the original tree or leaf nodes (corresponding to lexical items). Figure 3 shows some sample tree fragment pairs that were obtained from the example discussed earlier in Figure 1.

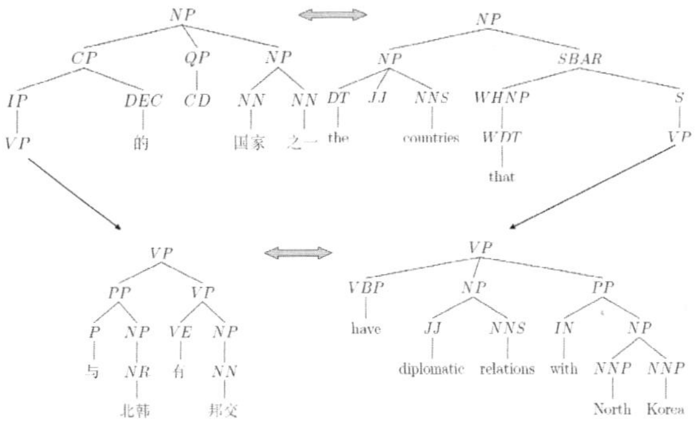

Figure 3: Tree Fragment Pairs Extracted from Aligned Nodes

5.3 Synchronous Transfer Rule Creation

In the last step, we convert the synchronous tree fragment pairs obtained as described above into synchronous context-free rules. This creates rules in a format that is compatible with the Stat-XFER formalism that was described in Section 1. Our system currently does not use the internal tree structure information that is contained in the synchronous tree fragments. Therefore, only the syntactic category labels of the roots of the tree fragments, and the nodes on the fragment frontier are relevant to decoding. This in essense corresponds to a "flattening" of the synchronous tree fragment into a synchronous context free style rule.

The flattening of the tree fragments is accomplished by an "in-order" traversal on each of the tree fragments to produce a string representation. Frontier nodes in the fragment are either labeled constituent nodes or leaf nodes of the original parse tree. These form the right-hand sides of the flattened rule. The positions of the constituent nodes in the output string are numbered to keep track of alignment of the nodes, which is often non-monotonic due to reordering between the source and target languages. Finally the root constituent label of the source tree fragment becomes the source-side parent category of the rule, while the root label of the target tree fragment becomes the target side parent category.

Accurate automatic transfer rule learning requires accurate word alignments and parse structures. Thus, to favor high precision (at the expense of some loss of recall), in our work to date on Chinese and other languages, while we extract syntactic phrases from all available parallel data, we extract rules only from manually word-aligned parsed parallel data. To compensate for the limited amount of data, we generalize the rules as much as possible. Elements in the rules that originate from leaf nodes in the parse trees are generalized to their part-of-speech categories, if the corresponding words were one-to-one aligned in the parallel sentences. Unaligned words and words that are part of one-to-many alignments are not generalized to the POS level and remain lexicalized in the final rule.

The phrase table extracted from the corpus and the rules are scored together to ensure that they are consistent when used in our translation system. For all Stat-XFER experiments to date, we have used just the source side conditionig with a constant smoothing factor for robustness to noise.

6 Extraction Applied to Chinese-English Parallel Data

We used the pipeline of PFA node alignment followed by rule extraction to build resources for a Stat-XFER Chinese-to-English MT system. The syntax-based phrase table was constructed from two large parallel corpora released by LDC for the DARPA/GALE program. The parallel sentences for both English and Chinese were parsed using the Stanford parser. The first corpus consists of about 1.2 million sentence pairs. Our extraction process applied to this corpus resulted in a syntax-based phrase table of about 9.2 million entries. The other data source used was a parallel corpus of about 2.6 million sentences, but many of its entries were from a Chinese-English lexicon. From this corpus, we extracted 8.75 million phrases.

Rule learning was performed on a 10K-sentence parallel corpus that was manually word-aligned, released by LDC for the DARPA/GALE program. This manually word-aligned corpus includes the parallel Chinese-English treebank of 3,343 sentence pairs. The treebank sentences come with verified correct parse trees for English and Chinese. The rest of the 10K corpus was parsed by the Stanford parser. The complete 10K parallel corpus was node aligned and rules were extracted as described in Section 5. Figure 3 shows two synchronous tree fragments that were extracted from the example node-aligned sentence pair in Figure 1. After generalization and flattening, we obtain rules such as those shown in Figure 4. The above process resulted in a collection of almost 100K rules. Some statistics on this rule set are shown in Table 3. Analysis of this rule set indicates that only about 4% of these rules were observed more than once in the data. These include the most general and useful rules for mapping Chinese syntactic structures to their corresponding English structures. Most of the "singleton" rules are highly lexicalized. A large portion of the singleton rules are noisy rules, but many of them are good and useful rules. Experiments indicate that removing all singleton rules hurts translation performance.

```
VP::VP [北 NP VE NP] -> [ VBP NP with NP]
(
(X2::Y4) (X3::Y1) (X4::Y2)
)

NP::NP [VP 北 CD 有 邦交 ] -> [one of the CD countries that VP]
(
(X1::Y7)  (X3::Y4)
)
```

Figure 4: Rules Extracted from Tree Pairs

Corpus	Size (sens)	Rules with Structure	Rules (count>=2)	Complete Lexical rules
Parallel Treebank (3K)	3,343	45,266	1,962	11,521
993 sentences	993	12,661	331	2,199
Parallel Treebank (7K)	6,541	41,998	1,756	16,081
Merged Corpus set	10,877	99,925	4,049	29,801

Table 3: Statistics for Chinese-English Rules

7 Conclusions

The process described in this paper provides a fully automated solution for extracting large collection of reliable syntax-based phrase tables and syntactic synchronous transfer rules from large volumes of parsed parallel corpora. In conjunction with the Stat-XFER syntax-based framework, this provides a fully automated solution for building syntax-based MT systems. The current performance of this approach still lags behind state-of-the-art phrase-based systems when trained on the same parallel data but is showing encouraging improvements. Furthermore, the resources extracted by our process can be used by various other syntax-based MT approaches.

References

David Chiang. 2005. A hierarchical phrase-based model for statistical machine translation. In *ACL '05: Proceedings of the 43rd Annual Meeting on Association for Computational Linguistics*, pages 263–270, Morristown, NJ, USA. Association for Computational Linguistics.

Michel Galley, Mark Hopkins, Kevin Knight, and Daniel Marcu. 2004. What's in a translation rule? In Susan Dumais; Daniel Marcu and Salim Roukos, editors, *HLT-NAACL 2004: Main Proceedings*, pages 273–280, Boston, Massachusetts, USA, May 2 - May 7. Association for Computational Linguistics.

Michel Galley, Jonathan Graehl, Kevin Knight, Daniel Marcu, Steve DeNeefe, Wei Wang, and Ignacio Thayer. 2006. Scalable inference and training of context-rich syntactic translation models. In *ACL '06: Proceedings of the 21st International Conference on Computational Linguistics and the 44th annual meeting of the ACL*, pages 961–968, Morristown, NJ, USA. Association for Computational Linguistics.

Declan Groves, Mary Hearne, and Andy Way. 2004. Robust sub-sentential alignment of phrase-structure trees. In *COLING '04: Proceedings of the 20th international conference on Computational Linguistics*, page 1072, Morristown, NJ, USA. Association for Computational Linguistics.

M. Hearne and A. Way. 2003. Seeing the wood for the trees: Data-oriented translation.

Kenji Imamura, Hideo Okuma, Taro Watanabe, and Eiichiro Sumita. 2004. Example-based machine translation based on syntactic transfer with statistical models. In *COLING '04: Proceedings of the 20th international conference on Computational Linguistics*, page 99, Morristown, NJ, USA. Association for Computational Linguistics.

Philipp Koehn, Franz Josef Och, and Daniel Marcu. 2003. Statistical phrase-based translation. In *NAACL '03: Proceedings of the 2003 Conference of the North American Chapter of the Association for Computational Linguistics on Human Language Technology*, pages 48–54, Morristown, NJ, USA. Association for Computational Linguistics.

Alon Lavie. 2008. A general search-based syntax-driven framework for machine translation. In *Invited paper in Proceedings of CICLing-2008*, pages 362–375. Computational Linguistics and Intelligent Text Processing, LNCS 4919,Springer.

D. Ortiz-Martínez, I. García-Varea, and F. Casacuberta. 2005. Thot: a toolkit to train phrase-based statistical translation models. In *Tenth Machine Translation Summit*. AAMT, Phuket, Thailand, September.

Arjen Poutsma. 2000. Data-oriented translation. In *Proceedings of the 18th conference on Computational linguistics*, pages 635–641, Morristown, NJ, USA. Association for Computational Linguistics.

Katharina Probst, Lori Levin, Erik Peterson, Alon Lavie, and Jaime Carbonell. 2002. Mt for minority languages usingelicitation-based learning of syntactic-transfer rules. *Machine Translation*, 17(4):245–270.

Yvonne Samuelsson and Martin Volk. 2007. Alignment tools for Parallel Treebanks. In *Proceedings of the GLDV Fruhjahrstagung*.

Stuart M. Shieber and Yves Schabes. 1990. Synchronous tree-adjoining grammars. In *Proceedings of the 13th Conference on Computational Linguistics*, pages 253–258, Morristown, NJ, USA. Association for Computational Linguistics.

John Tinsley, Mary Hearne, and Andy Way. 2007. Exploiting Parallel Treebanks to Improve Phrase-Based Statistical Machine Translation. In *Proceedings of the Sixth International Workshop on Treebanks and Linguistic Theories (TLT-07)*, pages 175–187, Bergen, Norway.

Dekai Wu. 1997. Stochastic inversion transduction grammars and bilingual parsing of parallel corpora. *Computational Linguistics*, 23(3):377–403.

Fei Xia and Michael McCord. 2004. Improving a statistical machine translation system with automatically learned rewrite patterns. In *COLING '04: Proceedings of the 20th International Conference on Computational Linguistics*, page 508, Morristown, NJ, USA. Association for Computational Linguistics.

Kenji Yamada and Kevin Knight. 2001. A syntax-based statistical translation model. In *ACL '01: Proceedings of the 39th Annual Meeting on Association for Computational Linguistics*, pages 523–530, Morristown, NJ, USA. Association for Computational Linguistics.

Author Index